Kicking a Ball
Down Havelock Street

By

Martin Mackarel

Published by Berrydale Press, Liverpool 2024

ISBN 978-1-3999-9469-9

Contents

First half!

Introduction

Chapter One	Street Football
Chapter Two	60's Football Legends
Chapter Three	The All Star Team
Chapter Four	Anarchy in the U.K.
Chapter Five	When Two Sevens Clash

Second half!

Chapter One	I Hate Students
Chapter Two	Work is a Four Letter Word
Chapter Three	A Bomb For Thatcher
Chapter Four	Get Thee Back to Yorkshire, Lad
Chapter Five	Not Born in America
Chapter Six	Frankly, My Dear, I'd Rather be in Kirkby

Extra time!

Chapter One	Ey, You're Yaphet Kotto
Chapter Two	Fatherland

Conclusion

Introduction

Havelock Street was once the steepest street in the Everton area of Liverpool, near where I grew up for the first twelve years of my life, although it is now long buried under Everton Park, a 1980s urban creation.

There are some phrases, Liverpool football cliches, I suppose, that were uttered when footballers made mistakes. For instance "'E' took the lace out of it!" when a player has apparently escaped punishment for a deliberate handball. This said, despite the fact that footballs have not contained laces for decades. When a goalkeeper has performed poorly, you might once have heard the words,"'E' couldn't stop a pig in a jigger", meaning that the keeper is so poor that he could not prevent the aforesaid pig from running down one of the numerous alleyways that still run between and behind rows of Liverpool terraced houses. Most damning of all was the comment that "'E couldn't kick a ball down Havelock Street", when the momentum of that hilly thoroughfare would mostly propel the ball of its own accord, if it were only on target. To be truthful, most amateur footballers would fail to kick the ball in such a way. Honestly, most of us are not that good. In Liverpool, most men and boys try to be footballers, but not many pass beyond the stage of the Sunday morning, youth or works teams.

Let's face it, if we were good, there'd be hundreds of British footballers in the Premier League, or at least capable of playing at that level, and there aren't. That level is so far above the average person, it's like standing at the bottom of a block of flats whilst the Premier player is on the top floor. So, I'll admit it - I'm one of the ones who couldn't kick that ball down Havelock Street. But I gave it a go. Like the rest of us, I gave it a go.

First half!

Chapter One

Street Football

I suppose that I shouldn't remember much about the sixties, since I was only ten when they ended, but I do. Most of all I remember the streets, where football was king.

Appropriately enough for a Liverpool fan, I lived in Anfield for that entire decade. The area in those days was thriving, with street after street of terraced housing, closely-knit communities where everyone was a character, everyone knew each other. For instance, in our area, there was "The Sniffer", who was constantly trying to detect gas leaks and using the pay phone in our shop to contact the gas board, and "Popeye", an old chap who spent his days in the shop reading *The Daily Post* and chewing on an unlit pipe. It truly was another era. The streets were paved with cobbles or a thin layer of stones and tar. Window cleaners carried their ladders on handcarts. Believe it or not, some deliveries were still made to the pubs with dray horses, and Victorian gas lamps still stood on street corners.

Those lamps provided a playground for generations of kids, as you could sling a rope from the cast iron side arm (designed to support the lamp lighter's ladder) and swing around on it for hours. When the lamps were lit at night, they caused little in the way of light pollution, so you could see the full panoply of stars on a cloudless night, a contrast to our mean streets. Then again, there was always the warmth, light and inviting smell from Frances' chippy, next door to our shop.

If you looked towards the River, you could see an infinite number of cranes lining the docks, signifying that they still thrived. The Barker and Dobson sweet factory pumped out a continuous stream of white smoke, which held a sickly smell, sometimes delicious, sometimes stomach churning, of Everton Mints and Chocolate Eclair toffees.

The streets that ran off the main road where we lived - Whitefield Road - were designated as "Play Streets". This meant that you could only drive down them if you lived in the street, despite the fact that each street conveniently led to a main thoroughfare, West Derby Road. The idea dated back a decade or two, before the advent of mass personal transport, at least in Liverpool. Children were, supposedly, allowed to play in these streets. As the sixties wore on and the motorcar became ever more popular, it became difficult to prevent your game of football being interrupted by passing vehicles. Towards the end of the decade there was a protest by parents about once a year, which usually made the pages of the *Liverpool Echo*. Surprisingly enough, most drivers did slow down and allow you and your mates to get out of the way, and they weren't even going too fast in the first place. Mind you, it was difficult to go fast along Celt Street, since half of the street had subsided to a depth about a foot lower than the other half.

One way of playing street football in those days was to get some chalk, or paint, if you wanted to be bolder, and draw a goal on the brick walls either side of the street. This is recorded historically in the film *Yellow*

Submarine. The cartoon Ringo wanders around a sixties Liverpool streetscape, that was not unlike the real thing, complete with a chalk goal. This type of pitch usually worked best if you weren't drawing or painting on the front of someone's house. There were some mums who just didn't understand football. Our nearest "pitch" was round the corner in Underhill Street. There you had the gable end of the terrace - conveniently the end property was a pub, "The Newbie"- and facing it the house belonging to the Friths. Old Mr and Mrs Frith were okay and didn't mind you chalking on their wall, maybe because their house seemed so much bigger than the others.

It was huge; they also had a yard next door with sliding gates, where the old man kept a 1940's "gangster" car and Willy, their son, had his Mk 1 Ford Cortina, which he'd customised in every conceivable manner. They sometimes let my dad park his car in there, if he wanted to keep it secure. When I was very small, dad even had a Vespa scooter which he'd take me for a quick ride around the block on. Willy was a mate of my dad's so, even though I was involved in the street games, I wasn't likely to get into trouble outside their house, if anyone did.

Football was of great importance to us as boys growing up in the sixties. It wasn't quite, as Shankly famously said, more important than life and death, but it did help to confirm your social status in the street. The trouble was, I've never been particularly good at playing it, but that's never stopped me. Most people are pretty hopeless at playing the game,
but a complete lack of footballing ability should be no bar to enjoying it.

In the sixties, the good thing was that I wasn't really aware that I was a poor player. Kids' football leagues didn't exist and my dad was not at all interested in whether I could play or not- he preferred rugby. But whenever a mate of mine called round, out we'd go, with whatever ball we could find.

The chalk goals on the wall were popular and served their purpose, but as Liverpool's slum clearance programme rolled on, open spaces became increasingly available to us. When half a street was knocked down, you suddenly had a huge football pitch on your doorstep. Trouble was that, even when the bricks were cleared away, you weren't left with much of a pitch. You still had to clear up stray piles of rubble yourself, but these could come in handy for goalposts. There were pits and hollows in the surface, the likes of which put into perspective today's minor complaints about surfaces "cutting up".When spring and summer rolled around, huge weeds and thistles, daisies and dandelions sprung up. Yet we played on these sites and considered them an improvement. Although, the balls we used didn't exactly help.

The most usual type was the plastic "fly away" variety. We used to sell these in our shop, particularly in summer. They really did fly away if you kicked them up in the air. A gust of wind would catch hold and what you expected to be your pinpoint, thirty-yard pass ended up coming back to you like a boomerang.

Or there could be other difficulties. If you were playing on a cleared site, the ball could go in any direction over the fantastically uneven surface (and sometimes we did as well). The vegetation that I mentioned could make the games interesting - one body swerve to go past your mate, then another to avoid the nettles. If your ball rolled into the street it might get run over by a passing car, but more danger was posed by householders, sick of the barely standing gable end of their house being used for target practice, coming out shouting choice phrases like -

"Will yer frig off, you little bastards, before I call the police!"

In true *Carry On* tradition, let's focus on balls for a while. If you didn't have a "fly away", you were reduced to a tennis ball. I've heard that Brazilian superstars honed their skills in this way, but to us it made no difference other than that you got kicked in the shins more often, as your opponent completely miskicked and connected with you instead. Sometimes kids would use a punctured plastic ball, and this was certainly popular in Underhill Street. Then there were the different grades of plastic ball. Most prized of all was the thick plastic ball complete with valve, which you could pump up when it started to become deflated. Most often, these were the Wembley Trophy balls. I've spent many a half hour attempting to pump air into one of those things, to no effect other than to end up a breathless heap. Above all these, and most prized of all, was the case ball. I got one for Christmas one year. It was the type that we used for football matches at school, made of heavy brown leather and tied with a yellow lace. Inside was a bladder, which by the sixties was made of rubber (it had originally been a pig's bladder, I believe.)

There were difficulties with owning a ball of this type. Firstly, heading became much more difficult. The balls, particularly when wet, weighed about half a ton, or seemed to when you were eight or nine, and if you did head it then your head and neck ached for the rest of the week. Secondly, they were no good for street football. The leather got scuffed almost as soon as you started to kick it about on concrete. With the cheaper "casies" the outer layer soon came off to reveal that it wasn't leather at all, just vinyl over a heavy fabric. Then again, if the ball was half decent, you ran the risk of having it nicked by a gang of bigger and harder lads who couldn't afford such luxury themselves.

The balls that were introduced for the 1970 World Cup in Brazil were light years away from the old brown leather type. They were made of hexagons of black and white leather stitched together and they were the precursor of every modern football since. That was the tournament that, for me, heralded the beginning of the modern era in football. Then again, I'm now quite old. A friend of mine once said that if you watch the 1970 Brazilian team apart from the fuzzy picture, they still look contemporary. Who came up with the idea of kicking the ball with both feet off the ground? Brilliant. I had one of those Mexico 1970 case balls as well. Still didn't make me much better as a player, though.

Liverpool in the sixties wasn't just about kids kicking balls in the street, of course. Both Liverpool and Everton had great teams that took it in turn to win honours each season. For me, of course, Liverpool F.C. was everything, and I suppose I have my granddad and Uncle Bill to thank for that. They were both football mad, and my granddad proudly held a season ticket in the Kemlyn Road stand. Bill had once, unsuccessfully, had trials for Liverpool, and played amateur sports - cricket as well as football -for many years. He'd often come into the shop and display his ball juggling skills. His favourite was holding the ball motionless on his foot for about a minute without it falling off. This was very good, since it was performed in the confined space of a newsagent and didn't involve kicking balls into jars of sweets or anything. This wouldn't have pleased my dad, who as I say, didn't like football, nor Bill.

I can't say that I recall Liverpool's first victory in the F.A. cup, in 1965. I was a little too young. My granddad had a 33 r.p.m. record of it, though. It included chants by the kop and some of the commentary on the game, which ended with Liverpool beating Leeds 2-1. I'd play the record on my nan and granddad's radiogram and wonder what half of it meant. I knew that Liverpool had won the cup and that it had involved a football match, but most of the rest of it was a mystery to me. I'd never been to a live game, which isn't unusual for a child under ten. I did know that I "supported" Liverpool and that there could be no other choice, ever.

There are some great footballing memories of Bill and my granddad from the sixties. At the beginning of 1966, he came into my grandparent's house raving about the forthcoming World Cup. He told us all about the mascot for the competition, World Cup Willy, a little lion dressed in an England kit, and he gave me a pencil and badge with World Cup Willie on them.

Again, I didn't understand completely, to the extent that I thought that this World Cup thing was always held in England. Why not? I certainly couldn't remember the '62 tournament. What I couldn't quite get to grips with was the fact that games in the World Cup were being played in

Liverpool. Later, in the summer, our shop, along with many others, was making a bit of money by selling World Cup Willie fly-away balls. Customers drifted in and out, my father asking them if they were going to the World Cup game at Goodison. The World Cup in Liverpool? Nowadays we associate the World Cup with exotic locations, but in '66 five games were played at Goodison, including a semi-final. North Korea was the team, surprisingly and incongruously, playing against Portugal in the quarter -final.

Apparently, they turned up with the wrong boots and little kit of any type, and the other teams pitched in to help them out. Despite all that, they'd managed to beat Italy to take second place in their group and were beating Portugal 3-0 at Everton's ground, in what has been described as the tournament's most dazzling match, before eventually going out 5-3. Eusebio scored four. If you used to mention the '66 World Cup to any male from Liverpool old enough to remember it properly, they'd think back and say,"Oh yes, Eusebio." There are probably only a few of them still alive.

My uncle Bill had a block ticket for all the games at Goodison and witnessed the "Cholymar" football team (the North Koreans) in their most famous match. According to an early 2000s BBC documentary, they modelled their style of play - very fast and energetic- on the spirit of recovery from the 1950's conflict in their home country.

That was called "Cholymar" in Korean. My granddad, apparently, didn't go to any of the games on the principle that they were being played at Goodison rather than at Anfield. As my dad said,

"Your granddad wouldn't have spat on Goodison if it was on fire."

Brazil, too, graced the city with their presence, although Pele was clogged mercilessly, (in a manner more befitting a Sunday league game at Clubmoor playing fields) being injured against Bulgaria and carried off against Portugal. I don't remember that game - just my disbelief that it was happening here in our city. Can you imagine the discussions that went on before that World Cup? The WORLD CUP- in Liverpool! In the present day, most fans can't travel halfway around the world to see the games, especially if they're in a faraway country. A in 2002, a conversation might have gone-

" Are you going to the World Cup in Japan and Korea?"

"No, I haven't got the money" or "There'll be too much violence."

In the summer of 66, what excuse could there have been not to go? A conversation in the pub might have gone -

"Are you going to walk twenty minutes down the road to Goodison to see Brazil, the World Champions, featuring Pele, possibly the best player the world has ever seen?" "Nah, I can't. It's the wife's bingo night."

Later, when England won, I was playing at Frith Beach in Prestatyn (not owned by the family from our street, I hasten to add) which was the nearest you got in the 60's to a theme park. I was with my brother Stewart, my Uncle Tom and his wife, Cynthia. Nick, my youngest brother, wasn't born yet. Tom was listening to the match on his car radio.

"They've won", he said. "Who?" I asked. "England," he replied.

"The score was 4-2".

"Oh", I said, and Stewart and I carried on playing.

So that was that.

Except for one more detail, a couple of weeks later.

On a rainy afternoon, late in the school holidays, I was in Liverpool city centre with Queenie, Cynthia's mum. Queenie was a little old lady who was always very kind to Stewart and I. In actual fact, she and Cynthia were not related to our family, but some ties are stronger than blood. Queenie was close friends with my nan and during World War two, my mum, nan and Bill had sheltered in her cellar, with Cynthia. Within the family, it was famous that Cynthia had dropped my mum down the cellar steps, as they were running to find safety from the bombs. Queenie had a valve radio which fascinated me, as it was marked with medium wave stations I'd never heard of, like "Hilversum."

Every week, she'd come into the shop and give us two shillings pocket money, until one week my dad told me,

"Queenie can't afford to give you that. Give it back." So, next week, I did.

Queenie was affronted when I explained my dad had said she "couldn't afford it", so I got to keep the two shillings, even when it eventually turned into 10p.

We went to the old News Cinema on Church Street, a place we often visited during Liverpool's year round drizzle. It was Church Street as it was in '66, before pedestrianisation, with traffic in either direction. The Tatler Cinema stood somewhere on the side where Primark and the entrance to Liverpool One are today. I wanted to see the almost continuous cartoons-this was in the days when children's television only ran for a couple of hours per evening, and only then in glorious black and white. The first thing that we saw was a newsreel of the World Cup final, in full colour. It was the one that was always shown, the Pathe News coverage. Queenie said something about not liking the Germans and,

"Isn't the Queen's hat nice?" and "There's Roger Hunt. He plays for Liverpool."

She cheered when the goalswent in, passed me sweets, and clapped when the Soviet referee said that the ball <u>had</u> crossed the line. We watched as the Jules Rimet Trophy was presented and Bobby Moore was paraded around, with Geoff Hurst and Nobby Stiles holding him up. Just before the cartoons started, Queenie came to the conclusion about why we won.

"It was the red shirts that brought them luck. The same as Liverpool's, you see."

Chapter Two

60's Football Legends

When we played football in our street or at school, there was no doubt about who was best- Nettie Christian. Her real name was Janette, but this was far too girlish for Nettie, as me and Alan Jones and the rest of the lads called her. Nettie could kick a ball, throw a stone and wield a cricket bat better than just about any lad in our school. Now, some may say that this was because everyone at our school was soft, but not so. I sometimes wonder if Nettie went on to become a WWE wrestler. If she'd been thirteen or fourteen, I suppose we would have considered her an oddity, but at nine years old she was just another one of "the lads", the Underhill Street gang.

I'd had girlfriends before mind you - when I was in the top class in Infants, I was quite the lad, with blonde haired Janet Minting and brunette Jane Hughes both vying for my affections. Jane was a nice girl, a homey type who really just wanted to look after me. Janet was quite different, and my favourite, much more exotic. She came from a theatrical family, her dad Roy being a well- known local magician and children's entertainer. Janet knew how to tap dance already and she had real charm. As football became more prominent in my life, however, I began to lose interest in Janet. I made a date with her one spring evening, promising that I'd call round to her house in Lombard Street and show her how to ride a bike, without stabilisers.

I arrived on time and Janet answered the door. "Just wait a minute", she said. I sat on the bike and waited.

And waited.

And waited some more.

I had no idea that Janet was "getting ready". Like most men, waiting for a woman to get ready has become part of life. We know it's going to be interminable. But then, I had no idea what she was up to. Had she forgotten that I was there? Had she decided to eat her tea instead? Who knows. I did know that I was getting very annoyed with Janet. After what seemed like a lifetime, but was probably more like half an hour, Janet emerged from her front door, wearing her nurses' uniform. Since each of us was only seven years old, I wasn't too impressed. If I'd been twenty- seven, and the girl had turned up for a date wearing a nurse's uniform, I'd have been ecstatic. I suppose that's very sexist, but that's men.

"Nurse Janet will now learn to ride a bike," she announced, walking over to stand next to me. "What do I do?" she asked.

"Well," I said, "you put your foot on the pedals like this. Then you take hold of the handlebars like this. Then YOU PEDAL OFF AS FAST AS YOU CAN!"

I left Janet standing in a cloud of dust. Needless to say, she never spoke to me again. Maybe I made a mistake. Last time I heard of her, sometime in the 1980's, she and her sisters were doing summer season in Llandudno as "The Mintings."

That was all in the past. Now, I was only interested in girls who could play football. The best place of all to play was in the park. We'd sometimes go to Newsham Park, the nearest one to Anfield, to play a big game. There'd be me, Nettie, Jonesie, and Mark and Noel Fox. This will seem strange to today's parents, but the park was about a half- mile walk away, and yet we were in no danger. Because of the distance involved though we needed supplies - crisps and a bottle of lemonade if possible - and this is from whence my popularity emanated. If my granddad were looking after the shop, he would regularly supply us with what we wanted. All we'd have to do was listen to his stories about how he'd made do with a bottle of water, and gone to school with his feet blackened and his toes tied together with laces to imitate shoes. It was only later that I realised he'd been taking the mick with that one.

The park provided absolute luxury - real grass, no bricks on it, just the occasional dog turd to contend with. You used coats, jumpers or a tree for goals. If there weren't enough of you to play, maybe you'd challenge another team. Then there was the usual argument about who was going in goal. No one wanted to. If you were an outfield player, you could pretend you were St. John, Roger Hunt, Ron Yeats. If you went in goal, who were you? Tommy Lawrence, the legendary "Flying Pig". I was amazed to find out many years later that American children actually find goalkeeper a glamorous, high status position. Apparently something to do with American sports mainly being played with the hands. In Newsham Park, the best you could get was someone being forced to play "goalie in and out", which meant that you could play in the outfield as well. What this usually meant was that, when the goalie was needed, he (or she) was halfway up the "pitch" instead. Sometimes this was deliberate, as the arrangement often was that if you let a goal in, then someone else had to take a turn.

This was all very well, but it meant that if the other side had a more permanent goalkeeping arrangement, then they usually won.

It was in this era that replica kits first made an appearance. They were light years away from what they are today. Even the kits worn by the professionals were much simpler in design, of course, but kids' kits were super basic. If you had a red top and red shorts, you had a Liverpool kit. If it had the white bits around the collar and cuffs, this was an improvement and brought you some status, until your mum washed the kit for the first time and the red ran into the white and made it pink. Possibly the height of kids' kits in the 60's was a shirt with a number sewn on the back and a club badge sewn on the front. If you could also add a pair of plastic Gola boots with moulded studs, then you'd really made it. These fashion items were not licensed products in the way they are today. You could buy the kits and badges cheaply in any sports shop, like the one on Breck Road. The boots were, I expect, more expensive, but a child could be kitted out relatively cheaply.

If you were really ambitious, you could get, or ask for, a second kit, that of another team. I'd always coveted the West Ham kit, but never got it. Instead, one Christmas, Stewart and I were presented with red tracksuits. I expect that our parents thought they'd done us proud, and in a way, they had. The nylon track suits had the same red and white stripe around the collar as the one worn by Shankly, and on the afternoons that we had football at school we came home for lunch and went back wearing them, carrying our boots. I never had any trouble with my "trackie", but in later years Stewart told me that he'd been kicked up the backside by some lads whilst wearing his tracksuit. Apparently, they'd gleefully shouted, in broad Scouse,

"Look! A taarrgit! A taarrgit!"

before booting him in the crotch and running off. I later realised that the stitching in the crotch of the tracksuits had been thoughtfully reinforced with some padding in a series of concentric circles. It did, indeed, resemble a target. Luckily for us, we soon grew out of those tracksuits. In the 60s, unlike the decades after, when it became a standard Scouse uniform, a track suit was a luxury, and attracted jealous attention.

It was about this time that I reached the pinnacle of my achievements in football at junior school. We'd been practising hard all summer in the park, and when school re started in September, Jonesie said he reckoned that, if he put in a good word for me with our teacher, he could get me a place in the starting line up for the 'B' team. Now, St. Margaret's wasn't a large school. It struggled to put together a half decent 'A' team, at the best of times. So a place in the 'B' squad was no great honour. However, it was to me.

We rode to the game, which was at another school, in a borrowed Transit van, sitting on the floor, proudly wearing our black and white striped shirts. We arrived, got out and were determined to do our best to improve the previous best result of the 'B' team- a 5-0 defeat. Jonesie and I took up our positions, twin central defenders. The teachers hadn't told us any tactics, or maybe he did and I didn't understand. This was, however, no matter. We'd made up our own tactics, during afternoons of shivering in the cold on Dwerryhouse Lane playing fields.

"Don't forget", said Jonesie, "we stand on the edge of the penalty area. If anyone comes up to us with the ball, we boot it away." It sounded like a good plan. And, basically, isn't that what professional defenders did in those days? Alright, they might have been a little handier with the headers than we were, but the tactics remained the same - get the ball, boot it away…although, to be fair, LFC full back Chris Lawler generally booted it to one of his own players.

At the end of the match our teacher, the wonderfully named Mr. Major, congratulated us.

"Well done, lads", he said. "That's the best result the 'B' team has ever achieved. You only lost 2-0. Who knows how well we'll do next time?"

The ride back in the van was jubilant. We were laughing, joking about the match. A large bottle of lemonade did the rounds. We looked forward to next time, when we'd surely win. Strangely enough, there never was a next time. The 'B' team never played again. Or, if they did, they never told me about it.

Of course, we weren't the real superstars. Liverpool F.C. was. Or sometimes Everton.

Both teams were about as good as each other, and kids at school were split about fifty- fifty on who they supported. Everton had Alan Ball, the World Cup hero, but we had Hunt, who'd also played in the England team. Hunt was a fantastic player, who held most of the scoring records for Liverpool before Ian Rush came along. It's surprising that he didn't score in the '66 final, as he'd scored three times already for England in the tournament, once against Mexico and twice against France.

Another memory about this time is of one of the first players I recall being transferred to Liverpool. Tony Hateley was to be our new superstar. A record £100,000 was paid for him in June 1967. Hateley started off well in his first season, but then he was plagued with injuries. The Everton supporters sparked up the chant,

"Tony Hately! Not worth a ha'penny!" in reference to the vast sum he'd cost. Any time I'd start saying how great Liverpool were, I'd get the "Not worth a ha'penny" chant from the Evertonians in reply.

I first remember watching football on television in 1968. Stewart and I were with my granddad and Bill, in a caravan near Rhyl, North Wales. Nick must still have been too little and stayed home with mum. Despite the weather being cold, grandad and Bill's first priority wasn't to get the coal fire going, but to fiddle with the aerial in order to tune into the cup final, Everton v. West Brom. Now, why two dyed-in-the-wool Liverpudlians like them were desperate to watch Everton, I don't know. Perhaps they were hoping to see them beaten. If so, they weren't disappointed.

Or was it just that there was a different way of thinking about football in the city in those days, a Corinthian spirit where the teams were rivals, but not enemies? Happily, that spirit seems to have returned. In any case, I remember being taken to see Everton's bus tour when they returned empty handed.

Again, were we there to jeer? I don't think so. In the same way, I applauded Everton's efforts in 1995, watching Amokachi as he held the cup aloft.

In the sixties, Uncle Bill had some connections with the club. Perhaps that's too grand a way of putting it. He worked for a company refilling vending machines and through this line of work had got to know Peter Thompson, the Liverpool winger who'd also had a few games for England, and some say was a very gifted player.

What was the link between Thompson and machines that dispensed hot coffee? Your guess is as good as mine. However, Thompson had a petrol station almost across the road from Anfield and perhaps they had coffee machines in there. The upshot of it all was that Bill, through Peter Thompson, got the entire 68 -69 Liverpool team to sign a set of limited edition drawings of the team for me. I still have that set and they're all there - Hunt, St. John, Callaghan, Emlyn Hughes, Tommy Smith, Big Ron Yeats, Geoff Strong and Alun Evans, the first £100,000 teenage player. Even the manager himself signed -"Sincerely, B. Shankly". That was the last good season for that 1960s team. In 1970, not only was there the wonderful Brazilian team winning the World Cup, but we also had Liverpool crashing out in the quarter finals of the F.A. cup. Who to?

Watford. That's who. Watford. I couldn't believe it.

When the news of that defeat came on the radio, I walked across Whitefield Road onto some empty ground where a row of shops had recently stood, now demolished. An old tunnel had recently been discovered, perhaps the work of "The Mole of Edge Hill", who'd riddled the city with tunnels as a philanthropic act after the Napoleonic Wars, to provide work, however pointless, to ex- soldiers. Perhaps it was just an old well, built before Liverpool stole its water from a reservoir in North Wales. The bulldozers were in the process of filling in the tunnel, but they'd stopped for the weekend and I looked at an iron bedstead that had been thrown across the hole to temporarily protect it. I thought about jumping in. The Evertonians were sure to mock. But I edged away from the hole and went in for my tea. I didn't have to worry. Mr Shankly righted things for me at the end of the season, dismantling the 60's team in order to bring in new players, like the dynamic Steve Heighway and, a little later, Kevin Keegan.

The sixties were great. Liverpool had come out of the second division and become winners, and a new team was on its way in. Also in 1970, I'd been to see my first game at Anfield. I'll try to describe how it was, but I must say I was overawed. Whenever I go to a match now, I still am. You come from the bleakness outside on Walton Breck Road, with merely traffic noise for company, into a blaze of light and colour, masses of people almost all of whom are there to support Liverpool, creating their own noise or drowned out by pop hits or L.F.C. related music on the speaker system. The pitch is very green under the floodlights, everything is heightened. That night in 1970, my Uncle Bill and Grandad had got me in on a spare ticket for the Kemlyn Stand, and the game couldn't have been more unglamorous - a third round, midweek F.A. Cup replay against Coventry. We won 2-0 and I was hooked. The whole thing was exotic, the cigar smoke, the swearing, the grown men shouting, the whole uncomfortable, fantastic, strange deal.

When I look back I realise what an absolute shambles Anfield (like most grounds) was in those days. The old main stand that faced the Kemlyn was made of wood, in a rustic, Mock-Tudor style. It looked more like something from a rural amateur stadium than something that befitted a first division ground. The Kop was just a simple terrace, at the back as well as in front. Even as a small boy, whenever I used to pass outside Anfield, I wondered how people didn't get killed - if there were too many at the front which led down to the pitch, then surely those at the back could get pushed down the steps which led back to the turnstiles. Couldn't they? But they never did. It took until the 80's, of course, for the major disasters that brought safer stadiums. The worst thing about the kop was the continuous stream of urine that poured down the terraces on either side during matches. (That, and the Boy's Pen, but I'll mention that later.) There were no toilets and this torrent of piss was, therefore inevitable, particularly when the Higsons ale had flowed freely beforehand. You were packed in with 24,000 others and you were lucky to be able to get to the top of the terraces in order to urinate down towards the turnstiles. Many made do with rolling up a match programme or *Football Echo* and using that to urinate as discreetly as possible. Others found that the backs of their trousers had suddenly, strangely, inexplicably, become wet.

Roger Hunt wrote an essay on the Kop in the 1968/69 season *Park Drive Book of Football,* or it was written under his name, which was rather more prosaic than my own recollections. Another sign that this was from a bygone era is the fact that Park Drive was a brand of cigarettes, which regularly produced football related publications. Hunt wrote that -

"While the Liverpool team has been acknowledged as one of the best in England and Europe over the past few seasons, we must take second place to our own fans. Bill Shankly describes them as 'The only professional spectators in the game. They have made an art of supporting a team and, by doing so, have played a big part in the success of Liverpool.' ... The Kopite is loyal without being bigoted. The Kopite is also aware of the part he plays in the success of the team."

Hunt may well have idealised the Kop, but there is no doubt that the atmosphere was terrific, in its day. He was probably right, the banter was wittier in those days, with less foul language than crept in during the seventies. A famous incident was when Gary Sprake, playing in goal for Leeds, mishandled the ball and appeared to 'throw' it into his own. The Kop burst into a chorus of the Des O' Connor classic, 'Careless Hands.' Another goalkeeper, Gordon West of Everton, would come in for similar stick whilst taking up position in front of the Kop. He was one of the first goalkeepers to bring on his gloves and hat in a small bag that was then placed in the goalmouth. I'm not sure if he ever brought the bag back to Anfield after the first time, however, when he got jeered with, "Where's yer handbag, Gordon?" All this was good natured and in better taste than some of the aggressive seventie chants, like the one to Tommy Docherty, who'd been advertising Gillette razors on T.V -

"You can stick your fuckin razor, stick your fuckin razor, stick your fuckin razor up your arse, SIDEWAYS!"

Another was the immortal (to the away fans)-

"You're goin' home in a fuckin ambulance!" This was chanted at almost every home game.

It was easy to be brave when you had 23,999 mates around you.

A few nights later my dad would drive my granddad home and I'd hear the old man complain about how terrible Liverpool F.C. was, even though he loved the club to bits.

To anyone old enough to remember the original Kop as a landmark of bygone, halcyon days, I have to say, it wasn't. It stank. Its time had come and gone and demolition was the best thing for it. There wasn't much that was romantic about having your leg urinated on. The current Kop is much better. It's even got toilets. And yet, if you drive or walk along Walton Breck Road on a match day, thing just aren't the same, the atmosphere both outside and inside has gone. Nowadays, you can sometimes even hear the players shouting instructions to each other on the pitch, in the same way that we mere mortals do whilst playing our amateur games. Silence wasn't something that you heard at Anfield in the sixties or seventies. My granddad epitomised for me the Liverpool fanatic of that time and my dad would often give him a lift to the match. I remember going with them, particularly to the evening games in winter. For the half hours before and after the games, the car didn't rule the road, the football fans did. They just walked along the road in their masses, and traffic could barely move. There was the obligatory hot dog seller, whose hot dogs and burgers came with a free case of botulism thrown in. Some say that the old Kop roof acted as an amplifier and certainly, when Liverpool scored, you could hear the roar from our shop in Whitefield Road. As you got nearer, the place seemed electric, the people pouring out of the chippies, the red and white scarves tied around wrists or necks, flags waving, people running. The dirty inner city street was transformed. I couldn't wait to go to another match.

"They're no bloody good, Liverpool. They should get rid of (insert name of player) and (insert name of player) is no good either. And the Flying Pig, he's useless. You mark my words, they'll be back in the second division before long. I think I'll get rid of me season ticket. Waste of bloody money."

He never got rid of it. Liverpool got their new team and kept on winning. For Liverpool F.C., the last year of the 60's was 1970. '71 would bring an entirely new era of football at Anfield. Skilful, educated footballers were on their way, footballers with mad haircuts and even madder sideburns.

Chapter Three

The All Star Team.

At the beginning of the Seventies, things in Whitefield Road were changing. More and more of the streets were falling under the onslaught of the council bulldozers, or rather, their contractor, Bache Demolition. Mr. Bache, or whoever owned the company, must have become a millionaire, since his lads were kept busy for a few years, destroying large parts of the city. At the time, some adults saw the clearance programme as a bad thing, and in many ways it was, because the housing that replaced the old slums wasn't much better.

My Aunty Gwen had already moved. Her house in Millard Grove had deserved the bulldozer's attention. It was a simple two up, two down. One of the back rooms was the kitchen. There was an outside toilet, but no bathroom, just the kitchen sink with a gas "geyser". This was a contraption dating from the 50's that you lit carefully with a match, then retired several yards while the blue flames heated the water in the cylinder above. You could even take a bath using this method, but first of all you had to bring in the zinc tub off the back yard wall, then fill it with bowls of hot water from the geyser. Finally, you got in, and, if you were lucky, the water was still hot.

It's startling to think that there were many people in Liverpool still living in this way, only at the beginning of the 70s. It's no wonder that Gwenie was more than happy to move to a maisonette on the grim council estate of Netherley, with its indoor bathroom, comfy living room and a kitchen with a serving hatch. On the other hand, we were holding on until the council made us a better "offer"- in other words, a council house in a decent area. I was beginning to hope that they'd hurry up. My old paper round was fast disappearing, as Whitford Street, Celt Street and even the more upmarket Lombard Street all came down. The bricks, rubble and empty houses were good to play in, but many of my friends were now moving away. Jonesie's family had upped sticks to Netherley. We'd been offered the house next door, but my dad wasn't interested. I couldn't understand why we were staying. The Whitefield Road area was becoming a wasteland, and soon there'd be no one left, except us.

The decade had started in a rather brighter way. It was time for another World Cup. There were the preparations and the build up - we were still World Champions, so who knew, maybe we could do it again. There was the team record, "Back Home", which my mum bought me at the record shop on Breck Road. That got played over and over again. Then the Park Drive rep. left another of his company's publications at our shop for me, *Sir Alf Ramsey's World Cup Guide.* There was a World Cup results chart at the back that I studiously filled in. I caught a bus into town with Queenie and came back with a World Cup magazine, detailing the information on all the teams, in full colour. Then there was the Esso Soccer Coins collection. My dad must have used some petrol that year, or , maybe he got the diesel for the taxi that he was now driving from an Esso station, because Stewart and I got the entire set. I still maintain that the collection is mine, but Stewart took it from my mum's house to his place some years back and I haven't seen it since.

The group stage went OK, although England weren't setting the tournament on fire. A one nil win against Romania and the same scoreline against Czechoslovakia. We narrowly lost one nil against Brazil, after Jeff Astle missed an open net, and Gordon Banks had made the 'wonder save'. On June 14th- the day of the quarter final against West Germany - my dad decided to organise a family outing to Blackpool. I was disappointed, to say the least, but family trips to Blackpool were nothing to be moaned about - in fact, I loved them, and we only got to go about once a year. I brought out the posters of the Liverpool players who were in the squad and left them downstairs for luck. So off we went, with my grandad minding the shop.

I still can't understand where we went wrong. My granddad broke the news when we returned, late on. I couldn't wait to hear.

"They were winning 2-0, the silly buggers, then ended up getting beaten 3-2."

There was no re-run of the game, or if there was, it was on too late for me to see. In later years I did see the game. We were cruising to victory at 2-0, the game was in the bag. Then we eased up as Alf Ramsey brought off his best player to save for the semi final and lost it in extra time. I had to console myself with watching the progress of Italy and Brazil. Cynthia and Tom came back from a holiday in Italy and they'd been in Rome the night Italy won their semi- final. They said that the cars didn't stop sounding their horns all night, people were dancing in the fountains as if they'd won the final. On Sunday, 21st of June, my dad was fixing his car in the Frith's yard. I went into their house to watch the final on their colour telly, the only one in our street. Brazil ran away with it. There was only one team ever in he match, and Boninsegna's goal was mere consolation. In fact, I don't think I even saw that goal. I went outside and watched my dad putting body filler in his Vauxhall Victor.

A little less than a year later, I was back at the Friths to watch the 1971 cup final, Liverpool vs. Arsenal. The build up to the game had been fantastic. I remember the semi-final, a derby game with Everton. It was a beautiful spring day. I was walking down to Ray's China on Breck Road to get my mum a present, either for Mother's Day or her birthday. I asked passers-by the score, hoping to find out what was going on, but no-one seemed to know. The game was being played at Old Trafford. I returned home to find that Liverpool had made it - a 2-1 win over Everton. Surely nothing could stop us from taking the cup now? The only problem was that we had to play Arsenal.

"I remember going to Wembley in 1950," said my granddad. "We got beaten then, so we'd best not be too sure." I couldn't believe his pessimism. We couldn't lose! I didn't realise that Liverpool had beaten Everton 2-0 in the semis in 1950, before going on to lose the final 0-1.

The morning of the game came in May. I had a Liverpool rosette, with a small F.A. cup stapled to the middle of it. We sold special editions of the *Liverpool Echo* in the shop, with all the build up to the game. *Shoot* magazine featured George McClintock and Tommy Smith on the front cover, as if leading the teams out on the big day. My dad let me pin the rosette up for everyone to see, so that they could give words of encouragement for the team. Hours before kick off, I was at the Friths, in front of their huge 24 inch colour screen.

As usual, the weather was warm and sunny. Wembley's turf seemed to be cut into an intricate pattern of stripes. The game began, and seemed to last a long time. I was eleven, and ninety minutes seems like ages. Then, Steve Heighway scored. Right, that was that. Our cup. But hold on, wait, what's this? A goalmouth scramble ensued at the Liverpool end and no one was quite sure who had scored. Maybe no one had, but no, the goal was credited to Eddie Kelly. Extra time, and Liverpool seemed to be tiring. Up ran Charlie George. I didn't like the look of him, with his long, greasy hair. A right bastard and a right Charlie. He kept on running, then let fly and scored that famous goal. I couldn't believe how such a thing could happen. I wanted someone to run onto the pitch and kill Charlie George, that's how badly I felt. I hated his celebration, lying there with outstretched arms, like some second rate rock star. To me, the cup had been rightfully ours. I hated Charlie George with a vengeance that only a football obsessed Scouse kid could. It's not difficult to admit that I cried as I returned to the shop that afternoon.

Still, the team has won a few games since then. And the 2001 Cup Final was finally sweet revenge for what happened that sunny afternoon in May 30 years ago. Mr Wenger, Arsenal's legendary manager, should not really have made excuses and blustered the way he did, for, no matter how much he was disappointed and felt robbed, he didn't feel as badly as I and thousands of other Liverpudlian 11 year olds felt in 1971.

Shortly after that momentous defeat in the '71 Cup Final, something else equally momentous happened. Primary school ended forever. Suddenly, it was the last day, we'd signed each other's home-made booklets, kicked the ball around the tiny playground one last time, and it was all over. I wasn't sure whether I'd see my old mates again, since I was going to St. Margaret's senior school, and they weren't. The senior department was a grammar school and it was six miles away, a bus journey that I'd have to make every day. Most of the others were going to Anfield Comprehensive. With us also being scattered by the demolition programme, would we ever meet again?

A good question, and apart from a few visits to Netherley to visit Jonesie and Auntie Gwen, the old gang disappeared. After a while, I even lost touch with Jonesie.

Secondary school was a long way away. I had to catch both the 27 Sheil Road Circular bus, and then the 87 or 82, which took me to Aigburth. When I started doing this, in September '71, I was still just eleven years old. A six mile return bus journey might sound a bit much to ask an eleven year old to achieve nowadays, but then, there was no question that you could manage it. Really, it was no problem. I never had any great difficulties. School football was more of a problem, though. After my dizzying achievements in the 'B' team, I was all ready to make my mark in the seniors. We all had to purchase our house shirt, which in my case was blue - not a good omen. In the first few weeks we played matches equally divided into house teams. Then the sifting process started. The school team squad was picked, the elite. Then the next layer, the house teams, who would play inter- house competitions. There were about fifteen boys left who couldn't play at all, and I was surprised to find that I was one of them.

This revelation amazed me. I was no good at football. After all those afternoons kicking the "casie" around Newsham Park, I hadn't even made the grade. I looked around me at my fellow rejects. We were all overweight or underweight, bespectacled or ugly. We didn't fit in and we weren't popular. We weren't local kids and we weren't from better class families.

Most of all, whenever we kicked a ball it went anywhere other than where we intended it to go. But, and this is important...*we had character.*

We became known as "the All Stars ". This was due to a particularly unkind P.E. teacher who thought he was being witty. In fact, he was a sadistic bastard who enjoyed slapping us for any minor infringement. In those days, most P.E. teachers had watched the film *Kes* and didn't realise that the cruel, bullying school teacher played by Brian Glover was intended to take the mick out of bullying P.E. teachers. It was satirical, but they took the character as a role model. They took every chance they could to make unkind comments about our sporting prowess. One of them used to stand in the centre circle and do a running commentary on our games, in the style of Brian Moore, a football commentator of the time.

"Here's Berry, running down the wing. He comes flying in for the tackle, and oh, he misses.."

Steve Berry was so fat that he could barely walk, never mind run. Hence the attempt at irony.

"And Mackarel goes for the header and collides with Smith.. these lads have guts.." Both of us were overweight. Funny,eh? Actually, he probably didn't say that. It was too witty.

To make the matches even more comical (if that were possible) the worst players got the worst pitch. Ours was right at the far end of the playing fields, with a pronounced drop to the right. At the bottom of the hill was a railway line, luckily for us not used in the early seventies (but which did later come back into service and was electrified.) It was lucky that there were no trains, since the ball would regularly be scuffed to one side, run down the hill and end up on the track. Then one of us would be forced to go and retrieve it. It went something like -

"Go down there and get the ball, Mackarel." "Who, me, Sir?"

"Yes, go on."

"But Sir, there's loads of nettles and barbed wire!" "Do you want 'the slipper' instead, Mackarel?"

"No, Sir", so I'd go and get the ball.

When the teacher asked if I wanted 'the slipper', he wasn't enquiring as to whether I wanted to put on some comfortable footwear and go for a kip. On the contrary, 'the slipper' was an old plimsoll which the P.E. staff took delight in hitting boys with.

They were allowed to do that sort of thing in those days. If they didn't have a spare plimsoll to hand, they'd just give you a smack around the head. Yes, we spent some great afternoons on that sloping pitch.

Many years later, as a teacher myself, I revisited those same fields. Amazingly, they seemed much smaller. The sloping pitch no longer seemed to exist. The school at which I taught was in a "scruffy" part of town and I hoped that they'd give St. Margaret's a footballing lesson. Sure enough, we turned them over five-nil. Not that I want to sound bitter. In fact, the "All Star" team was a great idea. I'm sure it must have been funny to watch a gang of boys who were hopeless at football, trying to play the game. Of course, the afternoons that stick best in memory are those when the sun shone, someone managed to pass to their own player, I managed to kick the ball upfield many times, someone scored and we won the game.

Those P.E. teachers may have been cruel, but in fact they were pretty much as sad as we were ourselves. A rumour went round school that they'd locked themselves in the teacher's office at the back of the changing rooms, during the annual "Fine Feathers" fashion show in the school hall. From there, they could take turns peeping through the keyhole at the models, as they got changed for the show. Is this true? Probably not, just teenage boys imagining what <u>they'd</u> do if they could get hold of the cherished keys to the P.E. office on that memorable, once a year night. Maybe it <u>was</u> true. So were the P.E. teachers sad people? Let's put it this way. One of them taught me French when I was in the second year. Despite being terrible at French, I got my best mark ever. My theory was that the teacher was as thick as I was; a theory confirmed a year or two after I left St. Margaret's, when I heard that he'd given up teaching French because he'd "forgotten it." He was going to concentrate on his P.E. instead.

Is there a universal opinion that P.E. teachers are thick? Perhaps so. When I was in my twenties and I'd go for drunken nights out in Leeds or Liverpool, if the taxi driver taking me home were garrulous, and wanted to expound on philosophical issues of the day, perhaps he'd ask me what I did for a living.

"School teacher," I'd slur, in the way that you can only slur after seven pints of lager. I was proud that I didn't in any way seem like most of the teachers I remembered… boring, respectable. I was trying my best to be the epitome of loutishness.

"Oh yes?" he'd reply, "and what's your subject? P.E. teacher?" Believe me, this comment was made many times.

****

By 1972, we'd moved away from Whitefield Road. One morning that summer I left for the last time from the shop and returned home to our new council house on Queens Drive, to find us all moved in. My dad had worked on the place for months, doing those home improvements that only happened in the seventies. He binned original fireplaces and replaced them with plasterboard or bang- up- to- date gas fires. Ceiling roses were removed and the ceiling covered with polystyrene tiles. Other changes were for the better; the hall was covered in cork flooring and given a coat of matt varnish. This hint of uncharacteristic tastefulness was offset with orange "flower power" wallpaper up the well of the stairs. The effect was finished off with brown "American Shadow" wall-to-wall carpet.

There's no doubt that the area was much better, and it was a vast improvement over the wasteland that Anfield had become. The only difficulty was that I knew no one, and Queens Drive, as the city's main ring road, didn't lend itself to playing football. Making friends wasn't going to be easy.

My saviour was the 60 bus. Lots of boys made the long journey across the city to St. Margaret's at that time. Inevitably, we got talking. One such lad was David James Melbourne. Dave was a real character. He'd become memorable during our school football matches because, at a time when the rest of us had little or no body hair, Dave could have got a job as an extra on Planet of the Apes. This guy made Tom Jones look like he had alopecia. By the time he was fourteen, Dave had a Tom Selleck style moustache. So Dave, in that decade when hairiness was much admired, stood out as a bit of a hero.

Dave liked football, and often went to watch Liverpool with his dad. Unfortunately, Dave also had a keen interest in something, which to this day, must remain the height of nerdiness, the Grand High Master of Geekishness. His passion in life was - BUS SPOTTING.

Now, I have to admit that I was becoming interested in this sort of thing. A deserted Whitefield Road, devoid of my old mates, had thrown me back on my own resources. So, I'd come up with the idea of 'plane spotting. I'd go and stay at my Auntie Blanche's house in Garston, and from there it was only a short bus ride to the airport at Speke. True, standing there for several hours waiting for planes to come in so that you can look up their numbers in a little book, then check what type of aircraft they are, is pretty sad. Dreadful, really. But at least the planes had some excitement about them. They were coming from, or going to, faraway places. The deafening roar of their engines as they took off was exciting, there could be no doubt. It also has to be remembered that, back then, most people didn't, or couldn't, travel by plane. I certainly couldn't imagine travelling in this way, to places like the Canaries, Corfu or the Costa del Sol.

Bus spotting was different. They were the stuff of everyday life. I'd travelled on hundreds of buses, and, as far as I was concerned, they were pretty much all the same. There was the new type, with doors on, or the old type, without doors, which in some ways were better, because you could jump onto them in between stops. Dave opened my eyes to the fact that there were, in fact, many and various types of bus. Together with his fellow bus spotters, they were compiling huge slide galleries of buses from the whole of the North West. Their hobby extended to Blackpool trams, as well. At school, they had a Bus Club, which was run by a Physics teacher, the King of the Nerds. He would organise the weekly slideshows where they'd drool over Leyland Lions and Atlanteans, rave over Routemasters and go ape over the number five tram to the North Pier.

It was into this hellishness that I was cast. I was the archetypal Billy-No-Mates, and here were some ready- made friends. At least Dave was OK. The rest of them I just couldn't get to grips with. They discussed f-stop numbers on their cameras, and looked forward to organised trips to bus depots. I couldn't make this stuff up - it actually happened. As desperate as I was for friends, I got dragged along on two of their excursions, to depots in Birkenhead and Manchester. Those days out were boring, so boring. Imagine my everyday existence. Go to school - by two buses. Get two buses home. What do you do in your spare time? Go on a bus journey to look at - buses. I attended the slide show meetings after school as well, but eventually it all got too much for me. I took to disrupting the meetings, using the sharp bit on the Physics teacher's Avometer (whatever that was) to point to girls that he and his cronies had inadvertently captured on their slides whilst snapping their buses. I'd use the pointer and shout things like, "The dial on you meter's going up, Sir", or ,if a particularly pretty female came on, I'd go mad, casting a shadow all over the screen, saying, "Sir, your meter's off the scale, Sir! It's in the red zone, Sir! I think its going to blow!" "Mackarel", he'd reply, "GET OFF ME AVO!"

He let me do this a few times. Maybe he did have a sense of humour after all. In the end, though, I got to him and I was banned from the Bus

Club forever, much to my relief.

To get back to football, let's once again turn to Dave Melbourne and his dad, Jimmy. I have much to thank them for, because I stood with them through many a-game in the early to mid seventies. David's dad was a funny little man with an intense passion for Liverpool Football Club. He was a proof-reader for a firm of printers, and read the pages each day as they trundled past him on a kind of production line. Jimmy's habit had been to rest his head to one side as he sat there, and his head had stuck in this position. Thus it was that I became a Kopite with hirsute David and his dad, head permanently cocked to one side. Jimmy liked to cheer for the team, as we all did, but his cheers were stranger than most. We'd be standing there, perhaps watching a dull interlude in the game, when Mr. Melbourne would raise his hand to his mouth, and, keeping it dead straight as if about to deliver a karate chop, exclaim, "Come on, THE 'POOL!" To make matters worse, all about us would suddenly be very quiet, and Jimmy stuck out from the crowd. Whilst others, including me and Dave, came wearing their Liverpool colours, Mr. Melbourne would be dressed in a raincoat and battered trilby hat. We always stood in the same spot, up at the right hand corner of the Kop, near the back, out of the crowds and the crush. Sometimes, when Liverpool scored, we'd get pushed down a step or two, but we'd always return to our rightful place. I sometimes wondered if he'd pinpointed the exact place to stand, right down to the last inch. On later visits to the Kop, right up to its demise in the early nineties, I'd pass that same spot and look for Dave and his dad, but I was looking for ghosts from another time.

They weren't there.

All this was a big improvement on one of my earlier forays to the match. At least with Dave and his dad, there was no doubt that I was safe. We'd walk back down Anfield Road and Townsend Lane, and catch the 60 home. Whilst still living in Whitefield Road, someone had convinced my parents to allow Stewart and I to go in the Boy's Pen, a comer of the Kop specially cordoned off for juniors. Perhaps my granddad and Uncle Bill took us there and met us at the end, but whilst inside, we were on our own. And if ever the term "Law of the Jungle" applied, it applied to the Boy's Pen. To begin with, we were caged in so well, with bars and barbed wire, that we could barely see. Then again, we were all quite small, and had to contend with thousands of adults' heads to peer over. Just as we'd managed *to* find a chink through which to peer at the game, the Hard Cases came over. Being very naive, I'd made myself a special hat so that I could better support my team. Left over in our shop from one of Liverpool's winning seasons, it was made of a light plastic in red and white stripes. To this, I added stickers of the players around the brim, early versions of the stickers that became so popular in the eighties and nineties. For someone who came from a fairly tough area of the city, I should have known better.

"Give me that hat", said the main Hard Case. His two mates stood behind him, In Case of Trouble. On my side, I had Our Stewart.

"He's got a 'Gimme the Moonlight' 'at", said one of the cronies, referring to a song routine performed by local favourite, Frankie Vaughn.

"No," I replied, "it's mine." I wasn't sure why I was being so brave, but it had taken me a long time to stick those stickers on.

"Give me that 'at", he said again. "That's my 'at."

"No," I again replied. A tussle started, and very quickly stopped, as the hat split in two, right down the middle. The Hard Case let go. He didn't really know what to do now.

"Oh," he said, and then to his mates, "let's go." The hat wasn't really worth bothering over anymore.

"Maybe we can stick it together with Sellotape," said Our Stewart. Nick was actually known in our house as the Sellotape Kid, as he believed that anything could be mended with plastic tape.

Through this whole contretemps, a policeman had been standing no more than ten feet away. He'd studiously kept his back turned the whole time. I went and showed him what had happened to the hat. He just smiled.

"Not much I can do now, is there, son?" After all, I hadn't exactly been beaten up. He carried on watching the game. Liverpool were playing Crystal Palace.

Later, as a sixteen or seventeen year old, I'd watch kids escaping from the Boys Pen into the main part of the Kop. Their heroics were often unbelievable; Steve McQueen would have been proud of them. They'd climb onto the steel roof beams and walk along them, then scale down the pillars that they connected with, into the Kop proper. Sometimes they just stayed up there in the roof, getting the best view in the place. To begin with, I couldn't understand their antics. Then I remembered my one and only adventure in the place where they'd come from. Maybe things had become even worse in there. The remaining inmates of the Pen would let out the occasional chant, in a high pitched, boyish tone-

"Ello, ello, Boy's Pen aggro! Boy's Pen aggro!" which would draw a laugh from the Kop. The Pen thankfully disappeared several years before the old Kop's fate was sealed.

I watched the 1974 FA Cup on television, again. I hoped that this time they'd do better against Newcastle than they had against Arsenal three years before. The whole of our family were gathered in our front room, and, this time, we had our own colour telly. The first half was tense, and both teams seemed to be doing equally well.

Alec Lindsay scored what appeared to be a perfectly good goal before it was disallowed. I couldn't believe it.

"There was nowt wrong with that!" I yelled. My mum went out to make tea. The second half started and the scores were level. The tension was mounting in our front room. Our Nick, still a little kid, hugged his Orinoco Womble. I was wearing my polyester imitation silk scarf, purchased outside the match for 30p. Suddenly, the game turned. Newcastle's resistance crumbled. Keegan scored from a Tommy Smith pass and we knew straight away that the game was over. The second came when Toshack passed it to Heighway. He changed direction and scored. Two minutes from time, and Liverpool players were passing the ball all over the pitch with ease. Keegan scored his second and that was that - three nil, apparently the biggest winning margin for some years.

I was overjoyed, despite the fact that I hadn't been at the game. At the full time whistle I walked outside, anxious to share my feelings of victory with anyone driving past, along Queens Drive. Maybe they'd slow down, sounding their horns, like Cynthia said that the Italians had done after their semi final victory in 1970. But no one seemed to care.

On the junction with Muirhead Avenue there was one solitary fan, a lad waving a flag. I shouted, "Hey!" and gave him the thumbs up. He seemed not to notice. I went to Larkhill shops and got ready to deliver my *Echos* on my regular evening paper round. I couldn't help but be jubilant. All the other paper lads were Evertonians, and they seemed to hang their heads in acknowledgement that, whilst Liverpool were enjoying a run of success, their team was now in the doldrums. Best of all, Dennis Law had scored the winner against his old club, United, a week or two earlier, meaning that they were relegated.

Later, while we waited for the *Football Echos* to arrive, I splashed out 8p on a bag of chips and shared them out with the other lads.

A few days later came shocking news. Shankly had resigned. Why? At a school where most of us were Liverpudlians, it was like someone had died. I remember standing on a staircase, waiting to go into a lesson. Dave Melbourne had told me. He always carried a little Japanese radio with him, to check up on the top twenty chart rundown on a Monday lunchtime. So that was it - no more Shankly. The end of everything I'd known. My granddad had always told me that Shankly was a genius, the man who'd reversed the fortunes of Liverpool, bringing them out of the second division and, in Shankly's words,

" ... Building them up and up, so that they become **invincible,** no one can touch them, never.."

After Shankly had bought Kevin Keegan from Scunthorpe for £35,000 in May1971, my granddad had returned to our shop smiling broadly, after seeing Keegan play for the first time at Anfield that autumn, saying-

"This Keegan lad's fantastic, and we got him for bugger all. Shankly's an even bigger genius than I thought."

Let's pay homage for a little while to Shankly's last great team from the early seventies. Up front, Keegan and Toshack, the Little and Large of the early seventies, spearheaded the attack. In midfield there was Heighway, Ian Callaghan, Brian Hall, Peter Cormack, Emlyn Hughes, Jimmy Case. At the back, there were Alec Lindsay, Tommy Smith, Chris Lawler, Larry Lloyd, and the young Phil Thompson. It was a good blend of youth and experience that took the First Division Championship in '73 and the UEFA Cup in the same season. They followed up the F.A cup victory by also winning the Charity Shield in '74, after a penalty shoot out and the famous dual sending off of Kevin Keegan and Billy Bremner.

After their double victory in '73 and again, after the '74 Cup Final, we decorated our house. Queens Drive is always on the victory route through the city when Liverpool wins a trophy. My dad, to keep us happy, made a banner, from wallpaper and red paint. We draped it outside, together with our scarves and posters of the players, even cardboard cut-outs of the cup, covered in tin foil. The banner read -

SHANKLY'S SUPER REDS.

My brother Nick still remembers that, as the open top bus went past, Shanks pointed to our house, put his hands together and applauded. Nick says that he wrote in his "News" at school next day-

"Mr. Shankly clapped at our house ."

The playing fields on the corner of Eaton Road and Millbank have for many years been known as the Bill Shankly Memorial playing fields. Shankly and his wife lived in the area, in a house that was comfortable, but on nothing like the scale that today's managers aspire to. Shankly in his later years would go out on those playing fields and join in with one of the kids teams that were playing there. No one was allowed to stop playing until his team was in the lead. Then he'd say he'd won, because he had to go in. Apparently, he walked in one evening and said to Nessie (Ms. Shankly), "We had a great game today, we won 19-17."

Can you imagine a Premier League manager of today doing that?

Chapter Four

Anarchy in the U.K.

After the summer of 1974, I'd given up football, at least during P.E. lessons. I'd had enough of being ridiculed for my efforts on the field. We didn't have to play football in the fourth and fifth years during P.E. lessons, so I didn't. Instead there were other sports on offer - badminton, table tennis, and basketball, anything but football.

Breaktimes were a different matter, though.

One aspect of football at break times that made life interesting was the outlandish clothes. We'd started off in '72 with trousers that were slightly flared. By the mid seventies, under the influence of the Glam Rock movement, the styles were ridiculous. There were 'parallel' trousers in the style worn by the pop group Mud, which started off at a certain width at waist level and didn't taper in at all. Shoes were equally silly. There were platform shoes with heels or platforms that had no heels at all, they were just one solid block of plastic. Together with our long hair and wide collared shirts, wearing blazers that had lapels large enough to have provided the wings for a light aeroplane, we must have looked ridiculous. Yet at the time, we thought we were super cool, and this was the fashion that you had to wear if you didn't want to be laughed at.

These fashions made football playing very difficult, to say the least. No one thought of bringing more sensible footwear for the break time games. You just struggled about in your platforms. Some of the more sensible lads rolled up their trouser legs to play, so that the massive flares didn't get in the way of the game, but most of us ran about with our flares flapping in the breeze, seemingly propelling us along, like the spinnaker sail on an ocean going yacht. All of this didn't matter. Our school uniforms, although they conformed more or less to the school rules, were imitations in black and white of what the stars wore on *Top of the Pops,* and that was what mattered to us.

There were new heroes now, like Ray Kennedy and Jimmy Case. We loved Jimmy Case. I remember discussing Case with Ray Low, another mate of mine who caught the 60 bus, and a football fanatic. Ray Low reckoned that Case was the best thing to come to Liverpool since his dad had started selling his famous Chop Suey Rolls at their chippie in the sixties. Stephen F. Kelly writes in his *Anfield Encyclopedia* that Case was-

"As wholehearted a competitor as you could possibly wish to have in your side. He liked nothing more than to power into the penalty area like an old-fashioned inside forward... Case had a ferocious shot.." We just described him, quite simply, as "Hard Case".

Another lunatic, perhaps even more aggressive, was Joey Jones, who joined the club in 1975. Kelly describes him in this way-

"Few players can have demonstrated the never-say-die spirit of Liverpool Football Club as much as Joey Jones....(he) played his heart out for his club and country." Jones' trademark greeting to the Kop was to run over to us and shake his fist aggressively in our direction, as if to say just he and the 24,000 of us were going to beat the other team single-handedly.

Ray Kennedy was different entirely. He relied on skill, not aggression. Me and other fans of the time will always remember Kennedy as a wonderful midfield player, dictating play and the pace of the game, but he had begun as a striker when he came from Arsenal, and it was Bob Paisley who converted him to midfield. Kelly agrees "It was always said that when Kennedy was on song, so too were Liverpool. It is impossible to overstate the value of Kennedy to Liverpool during the outstanding years of the 1970's"

I'd prefer to think of those years, from 1975-78, as the golden years of Liverpool Football Club. Not only had L.F.C. not declined with the departure of Shankly, they'd improved. Bob Paisley was taking them onto bigger and better things all the time, and when one of our best players left, two even better ones came along to replace them.

The Kop still sang the name of Shankly, but slowly, they, too realised that it wasn't he who was any longer pulling the strings, it was the quiet man from the North East who was the brains behind what was happening. Whilst Shanks had the charisma, Paisley didn't say much. He didn't need to. The team did the talking for him. I recently saw a photograph of his gravestone. It says, "He remained an ordinary man amidst extraordinary achievements." There is little doubt that Paisley's record will seldom, if ever, be equalled; in nine seasons, he won three European Cups, six League Championships, three League Cups and the UEFA Cup. Despite all this, he was only ever awarded the OBE, whilst those with lesser achievements have received knighthoods.

I was now big enough to go to whatever matches I chose, with whomever I chose to go with, or even alone. My first introduction to the real melee of the Kop had come during a FA Cup game against Manchester United. Even then, the famous rivalry with United had begun, although their glory years were still a long way off. The match was all ticket, and Uncle Bill had secured the tickets - for the Kemlyn Road stand- some weeks before. I was going, along with Bill, my granddad, his brother Sid and Sid's son, Roddy. I couldn't wait. Other lads at school hadn't got tickets, some had, but it was the nearest we got at that time to the fervour that is nowadays aroused surrounding match tickets.

Saturday arrived, we met up at my nan and granddad's bungalow and squeezed into Bill's car for the ride to Anfield. I was nervous as well as excited- I'd heard that United fans were head cases, intent on beating up Liverpudlians. Still, I was surrounded by family. We parked up and began the half- mile walk to the stadium. I remember being almost at the ground when Bill asked,

"Right, have you all got your tickets?"

Sid, Roddy and my granddad produced theirs, answering in the affirmative. "Martin," said Billy," do you have your ticket?" I didn't answer. My mind was miles away. Panic had set in, because the truth was that, no, I didn't have my ticket. Despite the fact that I was now a teenager, I still thought that adults took care of details like making sure that we all had tickets. I hadn't expected to have to look after my own ticket.

"Martin," Bill said again, "where's your ticket?"

"I.. thought you had it," I said. I looked around me at the faces of granddad, Sid, Roddy. Everyone always said what a bright boy I was. Now, this. Roddy looked at me as though I was stupid, Sid was surprised, granddad disappointed. He even turned away from me.

"It was on the sideboard in your Nan and Granddad's. Why didn't you pick it up?"

I said nothing. I could only think of the ticket, my ticket, lying there forlornly on the sideboard. It was too late to go back - Bill always cut it fine, and there were only fifteen minutes to go until kick off. My prized ticket would never be used.

"It's OK," I said. "I can walk home from here. I know the way. You just go in." Then Bill had an idea. It was one of his best ideas, ever.

"I think there's a pay gate for the Kop," he said. "I think they decided to keep it quiet, but someone said there's a pay gate. We should be able to find it." He turned to the others. "I'll take Martin in the Kop. Come on, let's go." He led me around the corner, away from the entrance to the stand, away from the others.

Miraculously, there was a pay gate, with hardly any queue. Once inside, Billy changed. He'd been a Kopite in the fifties and sixties, even, as he later told me, going to away games in outlandish places like Rochdale when Liverpool were in the Second Division. I'd only ever seen him in the Kemlyn, behaving properly with the other moaners, arriving five minutes late and leaving ten minutes early. Here, in the Kop, he became a younger version of himself, a real fan. At the top of the steps, I pointed over to the corner where I always stood with the Melbournes.

"Nah," said Bill. "You can't see anything from there! A waste of time. Follow me." He led me down, to a point where the steps levelled out halfway down the Kop. Then further down again, pushing past people who'd been there an hour, until we stood about a third of the way up, directly behind the goalmouth.

"This is where I always used to stand," he said. We were really in the thick of it -the pushing and shoving, flags waving, the various smells, the ribald chants and the miraculous mass swaying.

It was great. We were packed in like sardines. You could take your feet off the floor and not fall over. In fact, you had no choice but to move with the crowd - there was no other way to move.

Bill, to his credit, looked after me during the match, putting an avuncular arm around me if it ever seemed that the pushing and swaying was getting a bit too much. When Liverpool scored, the crowd moved down suddenly about six steps, then just as suddenly back up again.

"The secret," said Bill," is to avoid those." He pointed to the crush barriers, steel bars that were there for safety reasons. Whilst they may have stemmed the flow of the crowd to some extent, no one wanted to get jammed up against one of those things. If you got the weight of twenty people pushing onto you from behind, you had to be pretty strong to stand your ground, and I wasn't. I've seen grown men pushing back from crush barriers, desperately trying to get some space so that they could duck underneath or out to the side. Before games started, you often saw large gaps formed behind the crush barriers, no one wanting to get near them. All that happened was that, once the first push came, whoever had been in front - even if standing four steps back from it - got pushed down very quickly, directly into the steel beam. In 1989, this would prove the fatal flaw at Hillsborough.

In 1977 however, that game became a turning point for me. I never wanted to stand safely at the back of the Kop again. As far as I was concerned, I always wanted to stay where the singing was loudest, the shouting most aggressive, and the atmosphere thickest. We won that game three one and I was glad that I hadn't brought my ticket. It was a far different experience to sitting in the Kemlyn stand. Even then, I was tall and my legs were jammed up in the seats that seemed to have been built to accommodate midgets. Swaying and shouting in the Kop, my height was an advantage. From my new vantage point I could see everything, and when a goal was scored, I felt that I was really there- it was barely beyond touching point. This was the way to watch a game. In the stands, it was hardly any different to watching it on *Match of the Day*. Now, when I watched the replay of the games later the same evening, I was proud when I heard chants that had originated right next to where I'd stood. I wondered why I sometimes never heard the more lurid chants on telly - such as the one about Tommy Docherty's razor. I expect they turned the sound down on that one.

I never looked back from that point. If no one else wanted to go to the match, I'd walk up alone once a fortnight - it only took half an hour, after all. Saturdays were always the same, but always different. There were the same hawkers, selling badges, flags, and scarves. It betrays how long ago it was when I recall their cry,

"Thirty your scarves, fifty yer flags! Come on, lads, get yer Liverpool scarves and flags!"

The small enamel badges were best. If you wanted to be hard, you'd buy a Glasgow Rangers badge to go with your Liverpool badge, then wear them on the lapel of your blazer. This meant that you were a Loyal Protestant as well as a good Liverpudlian, in those sectarian days... the bigotry extended to Liverpool and Glasgow. The queue for the Kop shuffled slowly along, either at the corner of Kemlyn Road or along the blank wall that faced onto Walton Breck Road. Gigantic Police horses oversaw us, but the banter was usually friendly enough between their riders and the fans. There was never any question but that you'd get in- all you had to do was turn up and pay at the turnstile, buy your programme and find your spot in the Kop. All this for less than a pound.

The end of the 1975-76 season came and success was, by now, taken for granted. Sceptics said,

"The bubble will burst. Mark my words," but it didn't, and there was no real reason to expect that it ever would. Liverpool had won the UEFA Cup and the League Championship, and there'd been the traditional, now familiar, victory parade. My dad still decorated the outside of the house, but he was beginning to tire of it. His pot of red paint was running out. My mum's cousin John Holmes still turned up each year, to see the team bringing the trophies past. It was the only time we ever saw him, and I noticed the passage of time by noticing that John looked a little older every year. He'd begun as a young lad, sitting on the ice cream freezer in the shop in Whitefield Road. Ten years later he was beginning to get middle aged, but his scarf was still firmly jammed around his neck, his worship of Liverpool Football Club still fanatical.

I went on a foreign holiday with the school that summer, to Switzerland. Other than staying at a hotel run by the Swiss equivalent of Basil Fawlty, nothing happened. "Fritz", as we called him, had about as much diplomacy as the Luftwaffe pilots who dropped an incendiary on my granddad's bike during the War. One evening he berated us for our table manners.

"You English!" he stormed, "I think you come from ze jungle! You are like animals!" We whispered comments about the Waffen S.S., but didn't dare to speak. All this was over some food that one of the boys had shovelled back onto the serving tray, along with some untouched portions that our hotelier had been hoping to refry for the second sitting.

We made up for it all by sampling the relaxed Swiss attitude to teenage drinking. Lager was readily available, and we made the most of it. I recall that some of the tougher lads had been drinking on the train even before we left England. In London, they'd nipped off to steal some glasses for their cans of Long Life. For me, it was my first real taste of beer, and one that I soon acquired. Strangely, my spending money soon disappeared. When I got back, my dad asked me if there was anything left from the money he'd given me. I told him about the lager.

"Oh, pissed it up the wall, did we?" He left it at that. He was quite amused, really.

Returning to England, one of our trains was delayed at a station in France. Opposite us was another, similar train. It, too, was packed full of schoolchildren. I asked one of our teachers where the train was from, and after a few enquiries, he came back with the answer - Bruges, in Belgium. My mind clicked over. Liverpool had recently beaten F.C. Bruges in the final of the UEFA Cup. It had been a close, exciting game over the two legs, but we'd narrowly held on for victory in the away leg. The UEFA Cup had been one of the trophies that they'd paraded along Queens Drive in May. I went into Kopite mode, and shouted out at the opposite train, "Bruges are fucking rubbish!" It became a chant. In our compartment, two or three other lads joined in.

We chanted together -

"Bruges are fucking rubbish, Bruges are fucking rubbish... "

The remainder of our school party joined in. Little heads popped out of train windows. Teachers looked on bemusedly, as every single boy in our party now sang, at the top of their voices,

"BRUGES ARE FUCKING RUBBISH! BRUGES ARE FUCKING RUBBISH! NAH NAH NAH NAH, NAH NAH NAH NAH!"

Two or three other school groups, not even from Liverpool, joined in the chants.

The station rang with the noise. It was two o'clock in the morning and the place was reverberating with the sound of us, the English "animals", shouting our silly obscenities.

I don't even know if the other school children even were from Bruges. They just stared at us, uncomprehendingly. At one point, I asked someone,

"Does anyone know what 'Bruges are fucking rubbish' is in Flemish?" but no one did. We carried on chanting and they carried on staring. Then our train began to pick up speed, the noise of the diesel engines drowning *out* our row, and we were gone, heading for Calais.

If Switzerland had provided an introduction to lager, it did nothing to improve things as far as girls were concerned. Since that time that I'd pedalled away from Janet Minton, and left her standing there wearing her nurse's outfit, I'd had no success with the ladies whatsoever. The only lad I now knew who was a ladies' man, was Colin Hird. Everyone was jealous of "Hirdy's" way with the girls. He had blond hair, which was very popular at the time because of David Soul and Bjorn Borg, and a girlfriend called Julie. I knew Colin because of the 60 bus, again. In Switzerland, he'd tried to chat up some girls, together with Keith Sale and I. Keith was particularly plain and charmless, but supported Liverpool. Col's opening gambit was-

"Hello, girls, it's OK now- the talent's here."

I was so embarrassed that I turned away. I don't know how he got away with it- but he did. The birds were eating out of "Hirdy's" hand. He was wearing a snazzy, red plastic jacket, with a label advertising Malboro cigarettes. When I get back, I thought, I have to get one of those jackets.

Back at school and now in the sixth form, we had to endure something called General Studies lessons. Some of them were reasonably interesting, although the French teacher insisted that the idea was ridiculous and told us to play noughts and crosses or hangman instead, which we did. I spent hours trying to think of the names of obscure teams that no one would get. Few were fooled by Hamilton Academicals. Then our headmaster took us for a General Studies lesson.

"Now then, you young men," he started. No one was listening. Mentally, we were asleep. Only our eyes were open. "Now then," he repeated, "I'm going to talk to you today about... NOCTURNAL EMISSIONS."

The whole class suddenly jerked awake. Did he just say what we thought he said? "Yes, when I was a young man," he reminisced," I often had NOCTURNAL EMISSIONS. After all, your teenage years are the time of most need and least opportunity." We all looked over in the direction of Hirdy, then back at the headmaster. He was avoiding any reference to the words 'sex' or 'wanking'. Our head looked at the class. "Do any of you have NOCTURNAL EMISSIONS?" he asked.

We clammed up. No one was about to answer that one. I'm sure that we were all masturbating away furiously, but no-one was about to admit it.

"You may know it through the French name. They call it ' making a map of France.'" I wanted to tell him that nowadays, we call it a 'wet dream', but I knew that if l said this, I'd get ridiculed mercilessly. Personally, I hadn't had a wet dream for ages, since I was too busy wanking.

The head told us all about his teenage years, and I suppose we were supposed to take some comfort in the fact that he, too, had gone through his traumas as a lad. It was his way of trying to talk to us like young men, but to us, it was laughable. The class uttered not one word for the entire hour. In the end, the bell rang and he said, "No one can leave until someone has made a contribution." I stood up.

"Sir," I said, "Man is like a pebble on a cosmic beach."

"Thank you, Mackarel," he said, and we were dismissed.

I managed to get a girlfriend, of sorts. She was the sister of a friend of mine, and I considered her gorgeous. Unfortunately, I had no idea what to do with girls. I took her to see *New York, New York* starring Robert de Niro at the Odeon on London Road, and then, on another occasion, for pizza, despite the fact that we'd both had our tea and were full. The nearest I got to kissing her was a few clumsy pecks, whilst the "slowies" were on at the school disco. Then, I asked her the really important question, the question that burns in the heart of every teenage lad, everywhere.

"Susan," I said, "do you believe in sex before marriage?" She thought about this for a while, apparently seriously. "No," she said," I don't think that I do."

"Oh", I said. That was enough for me. I politely said goodnight and never saw her again. I still keep in touch with her brother. She's now a fluent speaker and translator of Japanese, and a would-be actor. She once auditioned for the part of Tinky Winky in *Teletubbies,* but only came fifteenth.

As 1976 changed into 1977, football was still the most important thing in my life. I was also dimly aware of something called "punk rock". I was told in school that it was horrible and to steer clear of it, but this only aroused my interest. The most popular music in school had for some time been "Progressive Rock" - the likes of Yes, Emerson Lake and Palmer and Rick Wakeman. So, no wonder that most lads were wary of Punk - it was so different. Paul Rickson, a new friend, told me of a club in town that was opening up, and that we could get in to see bands.

"A club?" I asked. "Don't you have to be over eighteen?"

"Nah", said "Ricko". "They'll let you join, and you can come down. Once you're in, you can get served at the bar."

I wasn't too sure about this. He said that they'd recently been to see The Runaways, an American, all- girl Punk outfit, and they'd had a great time. I asked a lad who he said had gone with him, Bill Cheng, and he said that yes, it was true. The club was called Eric's, and it was in Mathew Street in the city centre.

It was late November in 1976, and a little before my seventeenth birthday that I joined Eric's. The place was, it seemed. a direct cash-in on Punk Rock by Roger Eagle, a well known promoter who'd had clubs in Manchester during the sixties. Looking back, I now realise that there were equally as many non- punk outfits on the bill. Eagle had opened Eric's as a showcase for any good rock music, and it just so happened that the New Wave was breaking. At the club, they really weren't bothered about how old you were. It was Eagle's associate, Ken Testi, who signed me up- and I was wearing my school uniform. That was my introduction to the Liverpool Punk Rock scene. I went for the first time at the beginning of December, heard the Sex Pistols "Anarchy in the U.K." and that was it, I was hooked.

1977 was a momentous year. Punk Rock reached its zenith, and so did Liverpool Football Club. The first in a series of never to be forgotten matches came with the European Cup quarter final against St. Etienne. Word went round school that there was to be an early kick off, or that we'd have to get there early in order to queue up. It now seems crazy that such a game wasn't all ticket, but it wasn't. The buzz in school reached a high level of excitement. It became generally accepted that many of us would do something that I had never done-play truant. We weren't that bothered- we were in the sixth form, they couldn't touch us for it. The only problem was that the scale of the truancy was going to be so large that it would resemble a mass exodus.

Dave Melbourne had decided to leave school and get a job, so I had a new mate for going to the match, John Campden. We stopped off at our house in order to drink a "Party Four" can of Harp lager, left over from my seventeenth birthday, then made our way up Townsend Lane to the match. Everywhere, there were green flags, waved by St. Etienne fans. They had just one chant -

" Allez les verts!" Their green scarves were ubiquitous, and they were exchanging them, as we neared the ground, with Liverpool fans. Campden caught the spirit and yelled his own version of "Allez les verts," with an emphasis on the final 't'. A grizzled Kopite heard us and lent over to us with a word of advice.

"You two had better be careful", he said. Whether or not he mistaken us for French fans, we shut up. Campden, remembering his French, changed the chant to, "Allez les rouges!" The same idea occurred to everyone. For months, even years and now decades afterwards, the Kop would chant "Allez les Rouges!"

Queuing took a long time, much longer than usual. As we neared the turnstile, the pushing and shoving was becoming more agitated. I was pushed through the turnstile along with someone else, without paying, an arm sticking out behind me.

"Don't worry, lad," someone shouted, "that means someone else'll be able to get in now." The place was already jam-packed. I was glad to see that Campden was not far behind me. We teamed up again and went to find the spot that, by now, I always occupied, three quarters of the way down, behind the goal.

Campden and I had a great laugh that season, either before the game or at half time, by shouting out the name "Jimmy." Half the Kop in those days must have been called Jimmy, because, when you shouted that name, hundreds of heads would turn. We eventually got into trouble for that, later on that season, when some hard cases realised we were taking the piss. There was none of that silliness that night. The atmosphere was tense - at the other end, the Anfield Road was a mass of green, and it was the first time I'd ever heard another team's fans out-shout the Kop.

I recall the game as being the most exciting I'd ever seen. It's still talked about today, many decades later. To begin with, we were trailing 1-0 after the first leg, but we had no doubt that Liverpool would pull it round. Keegan lobbed one in after two minutes to level things, and that's how it was at half time. In the second half, it was more of the same. Liverpool would score, then St. Etienne would equalise. Bathenay scored theirs, for us it was Ray Kennedy. This meant that it was all level, but Liverpool would go out on the away goal rule. Then David Fairclough came off the bench. He was known as "Super Sub." A season or two before, my granddad had made me watch in amazement the television replay of a wonder goal that Fairclough had scored in the Derby against Everton. He'd taken on half of the Everton team before scoring. Could Fairclough do it again? The answer was…yes. With eight minutes to go, he ran half the length of the pitch, side stepped two defenders and slotted it home.

He'd topped even that memorable effort against Everton to overcome the French. The Kop was overjoyed, of course. Rogan Taylor, a football historian, has said that, when the Fairclough goal went in, he looked around him at the Kop, and "It was like a Heironymous Bosch painting." I hardly remember a thing, just the sheer, unbounded joy, people pushing, grabbing each other by the shoulders, waving their arms. It was bedlam in there for a long time. Looking back at the video, I can hardly believe that I was part of it that night, it just looks like one solid mass, not a collection of individuals. Liverpool had won 3-2 and we were in the semi-final of the European Cup, for the first time ever. "Allez les Rouges."

Next day, at school, we had to pay the price. The exodus had not gone unnoticed. A "kangaroo court" was set up to meet out justice to those of us who'd absconded.

Strangely, one of the judges was the P.E. teacher who'd taught me French years earlier, and had laughed at my efforts on the football field. We went in, one by one, not knowing what to expect. When it was my turn, I faced the P.E. teacher. He seemed bored by the whole business now.

"Well, Mackarel," he said. "You've been caught truanting. What's your story? Why did you do it?"

I looked at him quizzically. He looked back, equally quizzically. I wondered whether to tell him the truth, whether he'd then think I was 'one of the lads' and that everything would be O.K. between us, after all these years. Then I remembered his mockery of the "All-Star Team." He probably wouldn't even believe that I'd gone to the match, in order to witness one of Liverpool's greatest ever triumphs. He probably wouldn't think that I knew the first thing about football.

"Er.. I went home for me dinner, Sir." I said.

"But your bus pass doesn't start until three o'clock and you live in West Derby. How did you get home?"

"Sir, I walked."

"What, six miles?" "Yes, Sir."

"Why, Mackarel, why?"

"Sir, I, er..I don't like school dinners, Sir."

"You didn't go to the match?"

"No sir. no I didn't"

"Well, do thirty lines. Hand them in tomorrow. You can go, Mackarel. Send in the next one."

"Yes, Sir. Thank you, Sir."

I left the room. Later on, I compared notes with one of my fellow truanters. He'd played football for the school and had admitted that he'd been to the match. He'd still got the same joke of a punishment. I could see that the PE staff had been told to do this by the headmaster, and even they knew that it was all a farce. They were OK - just ordinary, daft men, trying to make a living. The same as most people. I saw the funny side of the whole thing.

Chapter Five

When Two Sevens Clash

I now realise that 1977 must have been a very busy year for me. I was attending Eric's club a couple of times a week, and visiting Anfield once a fortnight for every home game. Since I was seventeen I could now even go to away matches. Next up was such a game. It was the semi final of the F.A.Cup- again, against Everton, at Maine Road, Manchester. Strangely, many of my mates were now Everton fans. I'm not sure how this had happened, but it did mean one thing - my mate Smithy (yet another refugee from the 60 route) knew someone who was getting a minibus, and, for a couple of quid, we could go with them. I already had a ticket, due to my regular attendance at the Kop- I had the correct ticket stub - so going with a load of other Scousers, even if some of them were Evertonians - sounded OK.

The Manchester trip turned into a farce, not least because of the Comedy Scousers who formed the rest of our party. They were mostly grown adults, in their twenties or older, and obviously determined to live up to the image that Liverpudlians were now gaining as expert thieves.

We reached Manchester well before the game, but no one had any idea where Maine Road was. Someone had the idea of asking directions in a nearby taxi office. A good plan - taxi drivers usually know the area. Upon finding the office uninhabited, they came up with an alternative strategy. The dingy shop resembled the Marie Celeste, complete with a black and white portable telly talking away to itself. After checking to see that there was absolutely no one about, they did what anyone would do in a similar situation -nicked the telly. They slung it under a coat and carried it back to the minibus, where it was carefully hidden. Whichever team won, as far as they were concerned, it was Liverpool 1, Manchester 0.

The rest of the afternoon is memorable for the fact that Liverpool managed to get a 2- 2 draw, thanks to the dodgy refereeing of Clive Thomas (not that I'm complaining) and also for the fact that I lost my shoe. The days of platform heels were now fading, but slip- on shoes were in vogue. Perhaps I was too fashion conscious, because this is not the best footwear for standing on terraces. I had traded my ticket for the Liverpool end so that I could stand in the Everton enclosure with my mates.

This was not a problem, except that when Everton scored, there was a surge down the steps of the Kippax End, and one of my shoes came off. Now what was I to do? Hop back to the minibus? Luckily, the season was drawing to a close and the weather was mild. Still, the lack of a shoe was a problem. Liverpool equalised and the crowd stood still. My shoe was nowhere to be seen. Then Everton scored again and another surge, which I hopped forward with. When the cheering subsided, my shoe had come back to me, washed up on the return tide. With both feet once more shod, I watched the ref's dodgy final decision before Smithy and I headed back to find our Comedy Scouse mates. Given the allegiance of most of them, perhaps it was best that Mr. Thomas had only allowed Liverpool to draw, rather than win. The following week, Liverpool decisively won the replay, when in all fairness, it should have been Everton to have gone through.

This now meant that Liverpool was in the F.A. Cup final- again. As a schoolboy, I knew that I had little chance of a ticket. Yes, I'd attended all the home games, but the ticket allocation was based on having the correct stub and having it end in the correct number. Only then could you be lucky enough, and in my case it didn't happen. Then my dad suggested that he speak to The Sharps. They were colleagues of his on the black cabs (he'd switched trades completely since our shop had been demolished) and were related somehow to Jack Sharp, the owner of Liverpool's largest city centre sports shop. Perhaps through the company, they could get me a ticket.

The magic was worked. I got a ticket for the 1977 FA Cup final. Liverpool was to play our enemy, Manchester United. One slight problem was, how to get there? My dad had got the ticket but declared that, at 17, I was old enough to make my own travel plans. I relied on my old cohort from the 60 bus. I asked everyone - none of the others had been lucky enough to get a ticket. My last hope was Ray Low.

"Of course I'm going," he said. "My dad's taking me and David Rodsoe. You can come with us- there's room in the car."

Ray Low's dad had prospered in that decade. Before the days of Chinese takeaways where you could get just about any kind of Cantonese dish, plus chips and gravy if you preferred, Ray Snr. did well from selling basic Chinese cuisine in addition to the fish and Holland's meat pies which the other chippies served up. His chop suey rolls really were the best around and, for a working class family, they were wealthy. On the morning of the final, I arrived at the chippy about eight o clock, ready to set off for the long journey to London. I was surprised to see that Ray Snr. was in no hurry. Nine o clock came and went. Ray and his dad were packing pies and drinks from the chippy for the trip. I started to worry and my heart pounded.

"Shouldn't we set off now?" I enquired.

"Don't worry, plenty of time", replied Ray's dad.

By now it was ten o' clock. I knew that the journey to London took a long time - I'd been there before by road. Even by train, it took three hours. Here was Ray Snr. being completely leisurely about the whole process. At last, at about ten thirty, we set off. I was sure that we'd miss the kick off. The car that we were in didn't look particularly fast, just an ordinary saloon car. But then again, the only cars that I knew much about were the Matchbox and Hot Wheels variety I'd played with a few years previously.

Ray's dad got us onto the M6 and the strangest thing began to happen. He was a fast driver. From where I sat, in the back, I could see the speedometer. At eighty, we barely seemed to be moving, yet we were overtaking everything else on the road. In 1977, traffic was still a lot less than today. As the fastest thing on the road, we weren't even in the outside lane most of the time.

On the Ml, Ray Snr. started racing. His opponent was in one of those sports cars that I did recognise from my toy collection, a Porsche or Lamborghini. We kept pace alongside the sports car, until, with a wave, the other driver let us go past. What kind of a car were we in? When we finally arrived in North London, it was still short of one o clock. There was time for some lunch from the chippy supplies. Sitting down on a wall, eating a pie, I looked at the symbol on the back of the car- a

BMW. Never heard of it. Of course, I have now. I've even once owned a couple. I've since found out that the car was a 2002, capable of almost 140m.p.h., a top speed not much below the speed governed engines of today, which aren't allowed to do over 155. With the roadworks and traffic that we now have, I'd find it difficult to replicate the speed of that trip, even in a top of the range seven series, at the dead of night.

All that now remained was the match, almost an anti climax until I got inside. This time I was on my own, since the others had separate tickets. Wembley was vast. I seemed miles away from the pitch. The atmosphere was lacklustre compared to the Kop, but at least there was more space to move. In fact, the game seemed pretty boring until the second half. Stuart Pearson scored for United. I couldn't believe it. There were actually United fans in our area, celebrating. Strangely, no one said anything to them. Two minutes later, Jimmy Case hit one into the roof of the net and the place went wild. This was it! Now we'd win.

Of course, Liverpool didn't win. Jimmy Greenhoff scored a dodgy deflection -a shot by Lou Macari bounced off him and went in over the head of Ray Clemence. United had all the luck this time. Liverpool tried their best, Ray Kennedy playing well as usual, but it was no use. As I walked out, I wanted to cry again, just like in 1971.

Strangely enough, I saw plenty of others doing the same. Grown men were weeping. I didn't quite understand this back then, but now I realise that, if your life isn't that great, and you spend any money you have on following Liverpool, and the team is your only interest... when they lose a big match it's almost like the death of a family member. Or it was then. I can't quite imagine the football fans who attend today's premier league games being so fanatical. Maybe I do them an injustice, but the many out of town supporters who now attend LFC matches, speaking in Cockney, Irish or Welsh tones, perhaps lack the passion that those 1970's fans had. It was no big deal to them, to weep openly.

I met up with Ray Snr and the boys again and we were quickly back in Liverpool, stopping only once for petrol and meat pies on the motorway. When Ray's dad saw fellow supporters, they would share condolences, like relatives at a wake. I knew that Liverpool were in the European Cup Final a few days later, but now, I had less hope. Still, we'd already won the league again, a feat that seemed to give us little trouble in those days, so, who was to know.

I was back in my second favourite place on 25th May - my armchair in front of the telly, with all my family, in the front room. McDermott scored first for Liverpool, then Borussia Moenchengladbach equalised. Liverpool were getting the worst of the play during the second half when Heighway put a comer into the box. Tommy Smith, the old Anfield leg ripper, who was due to retire after that game, rose from nowhere and headed it in. Keegan was brought down near the end and Phil Neal scored from the spot, but who cared, Smith's header had been as sublime as it was unexpected.

The fans put all the disappointment of Wembley behind, as Liverpool became champions of Europe. Smith got a contract for an extra season, and after eventually retiring, did the after dinner circuit on the tale for many years.

What about my own football in '77? I've never enjoyed the game more. The sixth form had organised their own lunch times games on the school playing fields during the spring and summer months. We played on the old sloping "all stars" pitch, but without mocking teachers, it was a laugh. The old inter-form rivalries had disappeared, we took our A level studies at a leisurely pace. No one really cared if we turned up late for class after lunchtime. I lost weight, got fit and at least in my mind, played the best football of my life.

That summer, two things happened-I got a job working at a service station in the town centre, dispensing diesel to the taxi drivers, in the days before the fuel was generally carried by petrol stations. I worked night shifts and it could be lonely at two o' clock in the morning, opposite the Adelphi. The job wasn't nice, the diesel was smelly, but the drivers were entertaining, with stories of amorous adventures in the back of their cabs. In the early hours of one August morning, a cab driver pulled in and told me that Elvis had died. Given that cabbies are not usually the most serious people in the world, I didn't believe it. I was so disbelieving that the same driver came back later with an early edition of *The Daily Post*- the king was dead. He'd only ever loved football of the American variety, but still, I'd liked his music. Mind you, at 42, I considered him old.

By now I was seriously into punk rock. Even when my dad organised a weekend in London, and a trip to the Charity Shield match, I was more interested in going to Rough Trade records, in Notting Hill . I made him drive me up there, all the family had to come along, but being the teenager I was, I pretended I wasn't with them and told them to stay outside the shop whilst I went in. The game at Wembley - again, against United - I remember only for the fact that we sat directly behind the Royal Box. The game was a nil-nil affair, about as exciting as it sounds. My dad had obviously gone to a lot of trouble, again, to bring us here, and I wasn't even that interested. We tried to see who we could spot in front of us, but all I could see were hats and the backs of heads. They were really good seats that my dad had got, and I'd mostly acted like a teenage pain in the arse during the whole trip to London.

I was back at Anfield in August for the new season and a new signing. Keegan had gone to be replaced by Kenny Dalglish, a £400,000 British transfer record at the time. We soon saw that Dalglish was worth it - in fact, he was better than Keegan. I could sense the worry in the crowd at that first match - Keegan had been a hero of mine, and others, for the last six years. Dalglish soon became our new hero, and his association with the club would last forever. When Dalglish had the ball, it was pure magic. Or maybe it is just that it was so long ago, like the lunchtime football when it always seemed to have been warm and sunny. Of course it wasn't, there were rainy days, and some losses for Liverpool - they didn't win the league that season - but Dalglish, together with another inspired Paisley signing, Graeme Souness, formed the basis for the best team Liverpool ever had. What they did manage was to go on to win the European Cup again in 1978, making a feat that had once appeared almost impossible, seem easy. It was Souness and Dalglish who played a one-two to get past the Bruges defence and score the winner, the only goal of the match.

I never went to one of those European Cup finals - but I continued to go to Eric's. It was incredibly cheap to get in - an entrance price of 50p was considered expensive, for a member, which I was. Being such a regular I'd become a "face" on the scene, and I was enjoying every minute of it. I got to know Pete Wylie, who worked in Probe Records, around the corner in Button Street. This happened because I spent all my time hanging out in the shop, until the owner, Geoff, eventually started giving me cups of tea. I chatted to Wylie about music and eventually considered that we were mates, of a sort. That is, until I realised that

Pete's "mates" included half of Liverpool. I realised this when I once asked him to put me on the guest list at Eric's to see one of his early bands, Crash Course. He explained the problem; about 50% of the city making a similar request…the club had to make some profit on the gig. One time, I saw Pete walking down Whitechapel, near the old Silly Billy's hippy shop, with an entourage. An entourage, like Elvis! Twenty people, all punks of one variety or another, struggled to keep up with Pete's walking pace, and strained to listen to his every word. Some have speculated that, given Peter's motor- mouth style of speaking, he used amphetamines.

All I can say is that, unlike many of those I saw at University a few years later, I never saw Pete snort so much as a sherbet.

When I saw him with his followers, which must have been about 1979, I remembered 1977, when I'd met Pete at his house in Toxteth. It was smelly, damp and untidy. I thought it must be pretty cool to live that way, but it wouldn't be my first choice. From there, we got the 27 bus into town and sat on the back seat upstairs. The back seat was only for hard cases! I'd never sat in the back seat in my life, in all my journeys on the 60, usually because Stanley-knife wielding maniacs had generally torn it up. Pete sat there and, despite his short stature, unworried by the idea of *real* hard lads appearing, held forth on everything. I thought that only I was his audience, whilst, in fact, he entertained the whole of the top deck.

Wylie's connection to football is that he, too, loves Liverpool FC. George, the Anfield D.J., who has been there ever since I can remember, often played his song "Heart as Big as Liverpool" at the match in the early 2000s. Just how old is George Sephton? Wylie also did me the favour of introducing me to his other mates, who also hung out in Eric's and Probe at the time. Julian Cope had a big mouth and was a top poser. With another friend, Griff, they'd formed another early incarnation, The Nova Mob, and I interviewed them for a punk fanzine I'd started at the beginning of 1978, *Human Gladtidings*. Whilst Pete punned away, Julian thought it a hoot to stick the microphone down his leather trousers to do an interview with his penis. Their other mate in the group, Griff, had some T-shirts made, featuring an image of Jayne Casey, the singer with Big in Japan, later Cream's public relations guru and now, according to some, a Scouse icon. The image was taken from their publicity poster, only in the T-shirt version Jayne had been shot in the head, with a stream of poster paint depicting the blood.

When Griff came into Probe one lunchtime with the T - shirts, Wylie insisted that he give one of them to me. I was proudly wearing it a couple of days later, coming out of Probe, when Jayne was walking up Button Street towards the steps. I knew Jayne, not to talk to, but she'd seen me knocking about the scene for a few years. I still felt intimidated when she saw that T- shirt though - Jayne was the weirdest person in Liverpool in those days, with her mad eye make up and bald head. She took one look at the shirt, pointed at me and screamed,

"Who is that gorgeous person?"

before sailing past me into the shop. I'd like to think she was referring to me rather than the shirt, but that probably isn't the case. On his website I see that Julian Cope refers to those T-shirts as "his first release". My mum probably kept it in her airing cupboard for years- she never threw anything away.

Wylie's other mate at the time was Ian McCullough, and I also used to speak to him. He was about as shy as I was, and almost as young. He could always be seen walking through town wearing his raincoat, and for years would give me a nod as we passed. The most in depth discussion I ever had with him was in Eric's one night. He told me that he was forming a new band called Echo and the Bunnymen.

"You'll never get anywhere with a stupid name like that", I said.

I didn't really take that whole scene very seriously. I wasn't to know that I was in the middle of something historic. When Pete Wylie decided to pack in his French course at the University, I took his book back to the library for him, but not before I told him he was making a mistake. To me, all this was a lot of fun, but you had to go to University and get your degree, so you could get a real job. Wylie, though, was now mates with Joe Strummer of the Clash, who'd given him a guitar and, according to Pete, told him to "Pay me back when you're famous." I thought, well, yes, out of everyone I know, maybe you will get famous.

There was a big festival in Mathew Street that year, 1978, which was the total antithesis of the huge gathering that it has become in the present day. The "arty" crowd consisted of only a few hundred of us hip, cool people - or so we considered ourselves. That year's festival was organised by the Liverpool School of Music, Drama, Dream and Pun. They had an arty - farty cafe in there, the farty part coming from their penchant for vegetarian meals featuring beans and lentils. Years later, when only the cafe part remained, the legend over the door still read "O'pun". They were the first to put the statue of Carl Jung outside, the original one that got nicked. A few bands played that summer and they attracted only a small crowd. It was indicative of Liverpool's recent past as a centre of poetry that almost as many turned up the next day for the "spoken word" part of the festival. I saw local legend, poet and former Kirkby schoolteacher, Roger McGough drinking a cup of tea and sat through many amateur poets reading their stuff before I decided that poetry is neither as interesting as rock and roll, nor as exciting as football.

By now, it was time to go to University, to do some serious studying. One of the last things I heard on Radio Merseyside, on the night they played my request of "The Velvet Underground Live at Max's Kansas City" as the featured album, was that luvy dahling Julian Cope was forming a new band, The Teardrop Explodes. They needed a bass player. I'd been given one the previous Christmas and I could slap a few notes from it.

Should I give it a go? Nah, I was going to a glamorous centre of rock, football and fashion - Hull.

Second Half!

Chapter One.

I hate students.

The University of Hull in 1978 was all about disco dancing and anarchism.

I'd read about anarchism in *The Illuminatus Trilogy* by Robert Anton Wilson, and it seemed like a good idea. I'd gone to the well known socialist bookshop *News From Nowhere* and bought some books on the subject. My favourite was *The ABC of Anarchism,* by Alexander Berkman. I liked it for two reasons- firstly, it made me an immediate expert on the subject. Secondly, it was thin. For good measure, I took out a subscription to the anarchist fortnightly newspaper, *Freedom.*

I set out on my first day at the university by going to registration wearing a large badge stating "I hate students." I'd planned this for years, since being a paperboy at the newsagent in Larkhill, owned by a man named Neive. (I nicknamed him the Robber Baron due to the low wages he paid the paperboys.) He sold the badges, and I'd always thought, if I get to university, I'll wear one of those, just to piss them all off.

Sure enough, I was warned by the third year student behind the desk,

"We don't want any trouble out of you."

The masterplan had worked.

On the other hand, upon arriving in Hull, I was thrust into the milieu of student life by sharing a house with nine other lads. One lad was a Jamaican Londoner named Jonathan, who could speak both fluent cockney and patois.His instruction in the latter dialect has been helpful in dealing with certain students over the years, particularly in London. Being somewhat exotic,and a handsome lad, Jonathan was a magnet for the girls, so I tagged along in the reflected glory. Forgetting my anarchist principles, I accompanied John and his experienced, second-year mates on tours of Hull's nightlife. This was-

1. Romeo and Juliets. One in a string of disco clubs atop CoOp supermarkets. The beer was horrible and expensive, but it stayed open late.
2. The Bali Hai, whose main selling point was being named after a song from the musical *South Pacific*, complete with plastic palm trees. The students liked that classy touch.

This was our equivalent of New York's Studio 54, but in Hull, East Yorkshire.

Word was, the beautiful people hung out at the Bali Hai. I joined the Hull University Soul Club and added to my badge collection.

So what has any of this got to do with football? To discover that, we must follow the anarchist thread.

One evening I was in the student union, doing what everyone did at university in the late seventies- drinking beer and avoiding study of any kind. A scrawny youth my age was attempting to play the pinball

machine, wasting away his student grant, as he had no aptitude for the game. I had to laugh- he wore an anarchist badge.

"You know anything about anarchism?" I asked disdainfully. I was ready armed with my knowledge from the ABC book, and I took him as a slightly out of date punk rock follower who knew nothing.

The lad proceeded to spout anarchist theory demonstrating a depth of knowledge beyond even my erudite learning. He wasn't a punk rocker after all. He wore a jean jacket and ragged jeans, with a roll up cig hanging from his gob. This was a uniform that has never really changed for Neil, although he gave up tobacco in his forties, after he started turning the colour of a tobacco leaf and gasping for air. Now, in his sixties, he's a respectable, white haired, sandal wearing, south coast life long leftie, who enjoys nothing more than digging his allotment.

Back in 1978, he shocked me by sharing the information that he'd been arrested for a drugs bust at 17.

The newspaper clipping announced "Green fingered son went to pot!" At least he learned the skills to later become largely self- sufficient from his allotments.

A few weeks later, he showed me his dope stash, kept inside a hollowed out copy of a book called "Cause for Alarm".

"I learned that off the kids' tv show HOW!" he told me. "Keep your valuables inside a hollowed out book."

We now had two Hull university anarchists, and gradually, we found more. A mature student on my course, an acerbic Scot called Paul (whose favourite expression was "Ach!No.") said that he was a libertarian, which meant that he didn't like governments, nor anyone else, very much. Paul had a wee dog called Chummie, which was once quite accurately compared to a large rat. There was also Tom, who looked like, but hated, Leon Trotsy, and his French girlfriend Odiel,(who was odd in a French sort of way) and also Steve and Gill. Steve was a fellow Scouser who'd graduated already and worked in a high end hi fi shop. Gill was very nice, but I was a bit scared of her. I don't think she really thought that anarchism and disco dancing should mix. Tom hated Trotsky because all the far left groups hated one another; the communists hated the Trotskyists, the Socialist Workers Party hated the anarchists. One communist dismissed us as "liberals with guns", although the only ones we had were water pistols. That was, until one night when Big Stu turned up at Tom and Odiel's place carrying a rusty revolver, looking to get the revolution started. Big Stu was the original Hull anarchist, slightly balding with long straggly hair at the sides and a scraggly beard. He always wore army surplus combat fatigues. The story was that Odiel persuaded him to give her the gun, then, next day handed it in to the police. No one knew where Stu had got the gun, but even if he'd had ammunition, he'd probably only have injured himself.

We became the Hull Libertarian Collective, to accommodate Paul, whose opinion of anarchism was "Ach!No." Libertarianism has got itself a bad name as an instrument of the American far right, which hates the government regulating its shady and nefarious business activities. Back then, it was just a way to shut Paul up, and it made a nice acronym, HULC. We affiliated to the North East Anarchist Federation and, in an act of anti government direct action, Steve and Tom nicked a Gestetner reprographics machine, to print our leaflets, our call to arms in overthrowing the established order.

Then we retired to the union bar or a cosy pub for more comfortable evenings of jollity, paid for by our student grants.

On Sunday mornings, we'd get together for a game of anarchist football in Pearson Park. This was no different to ordinary football, except played solely by our Collective.

Tom was quite a dribbler, being fiery and tricksy like his lookalike, Trotsky. I'd try to get a tackle and usually miss completely. Paul would then come up and give him a good, no nonsense Scottish kick in the shins, at which point Tom would go down and reach for his fags for pain relief. Steve was often in goal, and would try to confuse us with surrealist philosophy. He'd also been part of the Liverpool School of Language, Drama, Dream and Pun in the mid 1970's and had attended the 1976 iteration with Bill Drummond, later of the KLF. He'd taken part in diving into a skip full of custard, amongst other jolly japes, and could casually drop a word like "atavistic" into a conversation without sounding pretentious. Steve wanted to rival Albert Camus, the French author of *L'Etranger* as a great philosophical goalie, but was probably dreaming of Linn Sonn Decks (the ultimate stereo turntable of the time) when the ball crossed the line.

Football and philosophy have been known to mix for a long time. Nowadays we have the professional pundits who wax lyrical about the game, and the armchair radio call-in experts. "After many years in which the world has afforded me many experiences," Camus famously said in 1957, "what I know most surely in the long run about morality and obligations, I owe to football." He saw the essential absurdity of existence in a game in which a ball is kicked about a field being turned into a global obsession. The Monty Python team recognised the philosophical nature of goalkeepers in their Yangtse Kiang sketch where goalkeepers write poetry about the most beautiful of Chinese rivers-

"Oh Yangtse!

Oh Yangtse!

Beautiful river!

River full

Of fish!"

~ Peter Shilton: **Leicester**

Of course, it wasn't actually said by the England legend. It was Eric Idle who made that up. A spoof Brian Clough, also voiced by Idle, then chips in-

"Well, you must remember, David, *er***, that these,** *er***, goalies -- especially Wilson, and on occasion Gordon West of Everton -- are romantics,** *er***, they're dreamers,** *er***, the Yangtse's a symbol for them,** *er***, for them it evokes,** *er***, David, a temple as well as a,** *er***, spiritual continuity."**

Bill Shankly, his words spoken by Michael Palin then adds-

"Oi, it's a... a river of many moods! To a young goalie like Peter Shilton of Leicester, the Yangtse is a beautiful river; but to a more seasoned goalie, like Phil Parkes of Wolves, it's a river of regret, of disillusioned ambition... and I think this is good."

Albert Camus further explained-

"I learned that the ball never comes when you expect it to," Camus once said of his time in goal. "That helped me a lot in life, especially in large cities where people don't tend to be what they claim."

Tom, on the other hand, was less of a dreamer and more of a technocrat. He got into the early days of home computing and owned a Sinclair ZX81, which was a super basic computer, but amazing in that it came in a box all ready to use- no soldering or valves required. It was an incredible change in computing, as the first computer I'd seen, at Liverpool University, took up an entire room. The last I heard of Tom, he was connecting up worldwide computer systems so that I could get my money out of my British account, from a cash machine in early 1990s San Francisco. I suspect he became either penniless or a billionaire.

The main opposition in Pearson Park wasn't other footballers, it was the dog shit. People hadn't yet learned to clean up after their dogs, and it was an "anything goes" approach. If your dog wished to shit in a field, on a path, on a pavement, no worries- go for it. Dodging dog shit was a way of life in the late 70s/ early 80s- no one questioned it.

Inevitably, I'd get dog shit on my trainers. Many times I had to trail back and employ an out of date copy of the *Hull Daily Mail* to clean off the crap. Finding some wet, long grass did help...it got the bulk of the offending article off. Hull's finest journalistic endeavour did the rest. One Sunday I'd turned up in pristine white plimsolls, purchased instead of trainers as the grant money was running low. The inevitable happened, and Paul jeered "away and blanco yer boots!". I've remained friends with Paul and his wife, Sue, for over 40 years, even though he is, at times, a miserable bastard. Then again, so am I.

Sometimes the football would devolve into a frisbee session. It was more anarchistic, as there were no rules, no winners or losers, just participants. Paul gave Chummie back to her original owner, and got a border collie, Machair, who he taught to play frisbee. We left the football behind and became the Anarcho Frisbee Faction. There was less chance of being caught by the dog crap- in the time that it took for the frisbee to arrive, I could do a quick scan for any lurking smelly brown matter. I'm not sure what their owners were feeding their dogs on back then, but it clearly wasn't good. I much preferred the white dog shit of my working class youth, a by- product of dogs being fed on mainly a bone diet, as these were free, or cost a few pennies, from the butchers. After a few days in the sun, white dog shit merely crumbled away.

When the New Romantic era of music came along in the early 80s, I once saw a group of posh students attempting to reenact Manet's *Le Dejuner sur l'herbe* in Pearson Park. I hope the area was suitably mineswept for canine excrement beforehand.

Around this time, I noted that Julian Cope's *The Teardrop Explodes* was coming to Hull to play the Wellington club. This was not a nightclub, more a working man's club that promoted pop acts from time to time. I dropped into the offices of student paper *Hullfire* and explained that I was best mates with all of the group, and could I get on the guest list in return for an interview. They agreed, and I turned up at The Welly and went straight backstage. Gary Dwyer, the drummer, recognised me and asked,

"Wharrer you doin ere?" and then added "where are we tonight?" I answered

"Hull" and explained that I was at the University and was looking for some memorable quotes. Gary told me to come back after the show when Cope would be around. I went into the main lounge and watched the performance. JC threw himself around like the pop star he thought he was now, imitating all his heroes from Iggy Pop to Liberace. It wasn't bad and Gary gave it a good go on the drums.

I wandered back to the dressing room. Julian was there and I said,

"Hello Julian."

In best high camp style, Tamworth's finest export replied-

"WHO are YOU?" I looked at Gary and he rolled his eyes. I gave a wry smile, shook my head and gave up on Mr. Ego, going home and writing a scathing review for the student paper. They turned it down.

"Why?" I asked.

"You can't say that Julian Cope is a pure egotist who arrived in Liverpool a year too late for punk rock, and nor can you say that when he sang, he sounded like he was losing a fight with the Boston Strangler!"

"Why not?" I asked.

"You were sent to get an interview with him, not to slag him off! Here's a Duke Ellington LP that came in. See if you can do a decent review of that, and if you can, you can keep it."

I shuffled off dejectedly.

Many, many years later I read Cope's own biography, in which he agreed that he'd acted like a spoiled twat, and was off his head on LSD most of the time. At the Green Man festival in 2017, Julian did a half music, half comedy set in which he ridiculed his younger self. He knew what he'd been like, and though the apology wasn't personal, I accepted it.

During my second year, Paul and I saw Hull poet and librarian Phillip Larkin in the off licence near campus. He was buying the cheapest gut rot whiskey on offer, as he was on a bottle a day habit by that time. At least I didn't have to listen to him sing.

Despite evidence to the contrary, (secondary school had finished after seven years) I thought three years at University would never end. I received a letter inviting me in for a career chat and along I went. I had little idea what to do with a degree in American Studies- it was pretty useless for employment.

"Do you have any ideas about a career?" asked the nice lady.

"Well, maybe I could be a teacher, but not the usual type of teacher. I could teach kids who don't like school, who are difficult, rebellious, and a bit different."

"Oh, like a sin bin?" she asked. I had no idea what I was talking about, as I'd just made it up on the spot.

"Yes, " I replied, "a teacher in a sin bin."

My friendship with Jonathan was helpful when I met one of his exes, a lovely lass from a posh Manchester suburb, and we started dating. Everything was free and easy in those days pre AIDS, so the relationship got fairly physical quite quickly. She was another Gill (an extremely popular female name at the time) and I was soon, I thought, deeply in love. I stayed the night at her parents' house over Christmas, and was stunned to find that there was a sink in the guest room. What incredible luxury! I put owning a house with a sink in the bedroom on my to do list for the future. Back at university, Gill decided that our deep love wasn't so deep after all, and went back to Jonathan for a while. I thought we'd been together for an eternity (it was about three months) so, heartbroken though I was, I responded by having sex with another girl I knew. As I say, all free and easy, and as Jon pointed out, "She was wiv me first, Mart." Fair comment.

Neil spent his third year in Lyon, France, as part of his course. I went over to visit, met some of his other friends, and it became a week of stoned football. We played in the local park until a parkie came over and asked if we were Americans. When we said, "Non, nous sommes Anglais", he told us to shove off. We played long balls from one side of the road to another on our way back from the bars, until we were stopped by the gendarmes. After showing our passports, they let us go on our way - too much paperwork. Neil was living in the school where he was a language assistant, and I'd bunked into a spare room. One late night, after inhaling heavily, we kicked the ball up and down the empty corridors. When the ball landed, it made a sound like an explosion, echoing so intensely I thought it could be heard all across the city…but no one seemed to hear. As Neil volleyed the ball back, it described a slow curve through the air, appearing to hang like a helium balloon, so ponderous was its speed. Then bang! It would hit the floor, and the echo would go on for minutes.

At the end of the week, there was a spontaneous game when some of the school kids turned up as we English- or "les ros bif" as we were described at the time- had a kick around in the school yard. It was England v. France and some of the twelve year olds were quite nifty. The score wasn't important (we probably lost) but it was handshakes all round at the end, and off in time for tea.

Now I had to sort out my post university plan. I applied to Liverpool University for a postgraduate certificate in education, specialising in English. I wasn't even studying English, but my desire to move back home and to help, as I explained, children to get the advantages in life I'd got (such as they were) was enough to convince the tutor to give me a place on the course. I'd only made one application and had got in. It was another year on a student grant and I had dreams of how great it would be to get my own flat and then maybe a job, but preferably no job at all, as I quite enjoyed doing very little.

My time at Hull ended with Liverpool F.C. winning the European Cup on a second occasion and a mediocre result in my degree- which, considering the amount of effort I'd put in, was what I deserved. As an aside, a year after I'd first worn my "I hate students" badge, they started selling them in the student union, and they became extremely popular.

Chapter Two

Work is a four letter word.

One thing I rapidly found out at Liverpool University was that I was required to attend every day. There was no more bunking off lectures; it was a small group of twenty or so, and any absence was quickly noted. I had to console myself with lunchtime drinking in one of the campus pubs, with one or two others who took the course less than seriously.

Fairly rapidly, it was time for my ten week teaching practice. I was assigned to a secondary school in the centre of an area which had seen the previous summer's riots. I'd spent that summer, when the disturbances happened, working in the diesel garage that serviced taxi cabs, as I mentioned earlier, and one light evening a driver pulled in telling everyone-

"Ere, if yer want a video, there's a feller drivin' round on a milk float loaded with them. There's mayhem going on up the road."

I was more worried about my teaching practice than I was about the riots, and even more so as at 22, I didn't even yet shave regularly. I bought some black trousers, a jacket and black Doc Marten shoes to look older and harder. So much so that on my first day, the kids were asking,

"Ey mate, are you a policeman? Which station d'yer work in- Admiral Street? Where's yer radio? Go on, show us yer radio."

They nicknamed me "officer." It could have been worse…it was just Scouse humour.

To begin with, I merely had to observe, make notes and write lesson plans, all of which would be scrutinised by the head of English, a humourless man in his mid thirties. The first time I had to stand in front of a class, I could barely speak. I mumbled and trembled so much, the pupils took pity on me. They liked that I was a proper Scouser, trying to have a go at being a teacher and an adult. Eventually, it became less scary and I gained some respect from the kids. I'd stand in the classroom and watch out the window, whilst bulldozers built what was to become the 1984 Garden Festival. They had a long way to go. I read stories to the first year children and one girl fell asleep, explaining later that she always fell asleep at story time, as her mum read to her at bedtime. The weeks passed and, after a visit or two from my university tutor, so did I. It turned out I was ok at the job. I was even confidently answering the staff room phone as if I actually worked there.

On returning to the university for the third term, I had one more essay to complete. I thought, I've done so well at the actual teaching, they can't fail me now. So, I didn't bother with the essay, and they failed me. I had to go to a meeting about it and was told to do the essay, which I did. I felt quite stupid for being overconfident and had to wait a full year for them to grant me the PGCE, during which time I couldn't be a teacher. Luckily, I could go on the dole and enjoyed more time doing nothing.

In May 1982, Liverpool F.C. won the league. Paul came over from Hull and we went to the match, finding it still easy to pay to stand on the Kop. It was 15th May and a warm day- all Liverpool had to do was beat

Tottenham. They'd started the season badly, and staged a comeback after Christmas. LFC won 3-1 and celebrated by throwing the trophy to each other, whilst jogging towards the Kop. Back at the flat, I played Mozart's clarinet concerto as a thunderstorm came in. I still associate that music with that moment.

There was something else I had to do though, which was to complete the 1982 Mersey Marathon. I'd seen the London Marathon on telly and thought, right, that looks good. I'll do that. It was April, and the marathon was in September. I sent off for a training plan and stuck with it. There were many late nights jogging around streets and eventually, out to suburbs I'd rarely visited. Sometimes the darkened and deserted roads looked like they'd hardly changed since Victorian times, as my footsteps echoed on the last few of Liverpool's cobbled streets. My routes were planned on a large street map of the city using a pair of compasses to measure the distances, as the internet was still years away. I could see all of the city laid before me as it then existed, and I ran the whole lot.

In mid September, very fit but only just about fit enough, I set off with a few thousand others to run from Speke to Bootle and back again. All went well until the 20 mile mark. I'd never trained beyond that. It was all I could do to get up the hill out of town, but at the top, on Aigburth Road, I knew it was all downhill. I could hear shouts of

"Come on, Taxifix!"

I was being sponsored by the diesel service station. People were encouraging the runners to finish, cheering us on in what was the first ever mass participation marathon in Liverpool. Almost at the finishing line, I spotted a lad from school, amazed that un- athletic me should be the one person to run the 26.2188 miles.

I got round in four hours and eight minutes, about nine minutes longer than planned and collapsed into a silver foil "space blanket". My great aunt Blanche, a Speke resident, was the only family member at the finishing line.

The next three days I could barely walk, and never ran a full marathon again.

I had a year to wait out and wasn't sure what to do with the time. I slept late and, once a fortnight, I cycled to the dole, still semi asleep, and signed on. I cycled back still in my zombie like state and went back to bed. My job at the diesel station turned into a job at a petrol station, which was far less lucrative as the drivers now pumped their own fuel, so there were no tips. Somehow, I met another girlfriend, an odd, hippyish but interesting young woman called Lillian. She wasn't the best looking girl but was quite compelling, mainly because she was slightly mental, which I liked.

Lillian was Germanic looking - like Steffi Graff but not as aesthetically pleasing. She was constantly ill, but her nuttiness was a challenge- I thought I could fix people. Eventually, that would turn out to be a mistake, but for the time being we entertained ourselves well enough, by living on omelettes, beans and yorkshire puddings. If money was really tight, we'd shoplift a bit of food from the House of Fraser food hall. Lillian lived not far from Manchester city centre on the Hulme estate. In the summer of 1983, we lay in her bedroom, listening to the old West Indian blokes outside slamming dominoes on the table, late into the warm nights. Our music was Van Morrison and The Dubliners, and the local pubs were The Ducie (where Mick Hucknall usually drank- he was a 1980s/1990s musician, kids) and the White Horse. The latter gradually lost letters from its name, firstly becoming the White Hor, then the White Ho.

That changed when I got a job back in Liverpool on a scheme for unemployed teachers. It was the days of *Boys From the Blackstuff*, and unemployment was so high that even newly qualified teachers couldn't get a look in. Liverpool University had finally given me my PGCE, so I took up the fifty quid, three day a week job. The role was in a drop in centre for adult learners looking to improve their basic literacy, and was based in part of a failing city school not far from where I'd studied. Business wasn't brisk, so I busied myself making fliers to advertise the place, and recruited another teacher to help distribute them.

One afternoon some lads came in, who turned out to be former learners who hadn't dropped in for some time. They were in their late teens, but were already beginning to look worn down by life.

"I used to smoke draw all the time, me," said one of the lads. "Y'know, Bob Hope, the wacky baccy. I'd get stoned and ride me bike everywhere. Not now though- I'm packin it in and trying to get fit. Yer smoke yerself, lad?"

"Same as you- packed it in to get fit." His mate piped up-

"Can yer ref us a game of five a side mate? That'd be great if yer could."

I promised them I'd do my best with the school, and they should come back the next day to check.

Sure enough, I got the gymnasium booked and by Friday there were eight or ten lads ready for the game.

It went well enough until one controversial decision. A goalie had picked up the ball outside his area, but his feet were inside his area. Was this allowed? There was a bit of arguing, but the ref's decision- me - was final. It's ok to grab the ball so long as your feet are inside your area. I had no idea if this was correct, until years later, on Match of the Day, I saw that I'd got it right.

I welcomed the lads back to our office for a friendly cup of tea and we agreed we'd do it all again soon. When they left, I went to put some money in our tea and coffee fund. It was empty.

"The cheeky bastards have had the lot!." Then we all laughed- even though we were only on fifty quid a week, their need was probably greater than ours.

I was brought down to earth around this time by an older couple who came into the centre looking for help with basic literacy. We went to a private room and the wife did all the talking. Her husband couldn't read or write a word, and now, even at his age, had decided to do something about it. Or, perhaps, she had ordered him to do so. I was completely overawed that this mature man would ask for my help, and became embarrassed and tongue tied.

"Er…I want to help…but I'm only 23.. I'm not sure it's a job for me…haven't been doing this long."

The wife replied, " he'd been through a war when he was 23, hadn't you?"

The man nodded. "Aye, joined at 17 and saw the lot."

I thought about this in silence for thirty seconds.

"Sometimes, there are more important things in life than reading and writing. I'm amazed at what you did."

The man seemed to regain his dignity and stared at his wife. They left in silence, and I never saw them again.

Lillian was discontented living in Liverpool, and I wanted to get a full time job. Not everyone can adapt to the city's uniqueness and individualism. She wasn't too impressed with my flat either, which was accessed down a back alley, and, needless to say, didn't like the cockroaches which came out at night. It was perfect for them, as the flat was warmed by a launderette beneath, and a pub to the side. I had a running battle with them using my Doc Martens, but they always won. Numbers were on their side.

I got a job teaching English at a school in Oldham, which would start in January. With my full time salary and Lillian working for one of the museums in Manchester, we moved to a ground floor flat in Chorton-cum-Hardy, a much nicer area then Hulme. All seemed well in the new flat, until we were kept awake at night by the sound of another couple having sex, the grunting and groaning transmitted in its entirety through the paper thin walls. I then realised that the flat wasn't much better than the one in Liverpool, as the builders had concreted over the damp course, causing black mould to build up at a furious rate. We complained to the landlord, who came along with some bleach and cleaned it, only for it to come back again within a few days. We had to do something fast. I applied for a council flat in Oldham, Lillian adding the entirely fictitious information that we had a tiny baby. We immediately went to the top of the list and got a flat in Hathershaw, on a run down estate. I was certain I could fix up the flat, and the council offered money off the rent if I did so. Days were spent at the school and nights at the flat, before bussing it back to Manchester to do it all again the next day. Any book marking I did was on the forty five minute journey, and a couple of times I caught myself dozing off. Eventually, working on the flat at weekends as well, and with my dad and Uncle Bill lending as hand, the flat was decent enough to move in. My dad used the opportunity to show that he was still strong, carrying the cast iron gas stove up the steps on his back.

Our next door neighbours were an old couple, a retired miner called Ron, and his wife, Martha.

We brought our furniture in through a typical Oldham snowstorm sometime in early February.

"Welcome to winter wonderland," said Ron.

It was well…down to earth, to be kind. We did it up further, with Habitat lampshades and curtains, and there was a park just around the corner. This was usually full of parents playing with small children, and teenagers sniffing glue. Everyday, a pack of stray dogs roamed the estate. Lillian gave me a book to read, *Hard Living on Clay Street: Portraits of Blue Collar Families*, by Joseph T Howard. It was an American book.

"I didn't need to read this", I said after finishing it. "I'm living this right now."

The job at the secondary school wasn't going all that well. It was a job, certainly, but many of the students and parents seemed middle class and entitled. Classes were "mixed ability" and the theory was that osmosis would cause a transfer of intelligence from the more to the less intelligent. Kids who needed extra help didn't get it, and some of the more able took to messing about whilst I helped the strugglers. There were two young women teachers my age in the department, and I could see that they were doing better than I was. I fancied one of these two quite desperately and I could see she felt the same, but I went ahead and married Lillian in the summer, and the girl followed suit and married her boyfriend soon afterwards. Did everyone marry very young in the early 1980s? I was twenty four years old but felt fifty.

The job was only temporary and I left at the end of the year. The headmaster, a pompous man who sat in his office all day sending out edicts, wished me farewell with a cheap bottle of plonk.

He didn't ask me if I had a few words to say, but I said them anyway.

"It's untrue to say that I owe the school nothing. I owe it £2.35 for personal phone calls. Headmaster, here is your cheque." I got a great laugh from the staff and walked out. Fight the power, man.

Chapter Three

A bomb for Thatcher

"A bomb went off to deadly effect in 1984 at a hotel in Brighton, England, where members of Britain's Conservative Party were gathered for a conference." News report, October 1984.

I was doing supply teaching at a High School in North Manchester when this news came through on the morning of 12th October. Teachers, in those days, were a fairly bolshy and left wing lot. There were many Guardian readers, leather elbow patches and beards being popular amongst the blokes, and dangly earrings, Greenham Common badges and long skirts being the style for the women, so there was an atmosphere of rejoicing at the possibility that Thatcher had been blown up. When we found out she'd survived, it was a bit of a downer, but we had the day to crack on with.

I'd gone to the school to teach English, but when they realised I was a young man, I was quickly transferred to P.E. duties. My mum had sown my Mersey Marathon patch onto my trackie top, and I thought I really looked the part, just like the 1970s P.E. teachers I'd known and hated. With a whistle round my neck I was loving it, telling the lads to do this, do that, get changed quicker, hurry up, it's time for yer next lesson, etc.

I was doing one P.E. a lesson in the hall when a weatherbeaten female teacher walked in and visually scanned the place. Addressing me, she said,

"Where's your teacher?"

"Er, it's me. I'm the teacher." She looked me up and down and said-

"Oh" and walked off. It was proof of the adage that, when the teachers start looking young, you know you're getting old. Eventually, that feeling would come to me.

In fact, I was doing so well at referring the football that, at the end of the week, the head of P.E., a man who looked a veteran of many hard tackles and January days on muddy fields, stated-

"I think this lad deserves the Golden Whistle Award."

I knew he was joking, but I was quite pleased. Next day I was told that the absent teacher would be back, and my services were no longer required. It was tough.

No matter though, as almost immediately, I got a long term job teaching English and maths at a Community School on the Langley estate in Rochdale. The estate had been built, like Kirkby in Merseyside, to house the people from working class areas of Manchester. By the 1980s, it was in decline, and so was the school. The local people were fighting back, though. The school had an art gallery and the local shops and some houses were being refurbished. Sadly, there was no money to fix up the school, and when it rained, the buckets came out.

I was to teach the special needs, or "remedial class" kids, working on their basic skills. The main thing for me to remember was - there's no money, and they're unruly. I put my Dr. Marten shoes back on (I still had them) and got to work. Luckily, the art department was next door and they were two of the best teachers I'd ever met, full of joviality and they loved what they did. There was no budget for paper, so the pupils painted and drew on the backs of wallpaper samples. I had no experience in maths, so as well as worksheets, I got the kids making copies of maths posters that we couldn't afford to buy. I learned about tessellations and we created our own, using boxes of shapes I found. The kids wrote stories and I wrote stories about UFOs and ghosts to read to them. They were a difficult audience who had their problems. More should have been done for some of them, but although I voiced a little concern to the deputy head,the policy at the time was not to intervene…very different to now.

To improve my positive relationship with the pupils, I asked the head of P.E. if I could run after school five- a- side sessions. He said it was OK, I could do what I liked, and just remember to let the caretaker know when we'd finished. So a 24 year old teacher, who hadn't even finished his probationary teaching, was left alone with a group of lads. I had this. No problem.

The five-a-side proved popular and more kids came along each week. I'd play and referee in the games, taking my own turn emulating Mr. Sugden from the film *Kes,* played brilliantly by Brian Glover. I did try to be a bit fairer than Sugden, and it all went well for a month or so. I became so confident in my own ability that I became quite lively in the games, until one large lad followed through with an enthusiastic tackle, and caught me on the shin. The pain was quite intense and if I look closely, I can still see the scar on my leg, decades later.

"That FUCKIN HURT!" I shouted, losing the plot.

The gymnasium was in an uproar. Kids who'd been sitting atop the wall bars (not a problem in the 80s) shouted and swore back at me.

"Teachers don't swear!" said one vocal youth. I'd broken the illusion of being a teacher, I'd acted unprofessionally, and the kids did not like it.

Somehow, and I can't remember how, I cleared them all out of the school and things calmed down, but I was mortified by my error. Next day, I apologised to the head of P.E., another veteran, although, at that stage almost everyone looked like a veteran.

"Don't worry", he said. "If this place crumbled a bit every time someone swore, it'd be a heap of dust by now."

I was impressed by his philosophical approach. Must have been a goalkeeper, I thought.

Christmas 1984 was approaching, and Lillian now had a job organising the Christmas festivities in Manchester City Centre. Most impressively, the city had purchased a giant inflatable Santa Claus, and attached him halfway up the tower of Manchester Town Hall. Lillian and her colleagues had worked hard getting shops and businesses to donate to the Christmas lights and decorations in their streets, so we were both invited to the official illuminations switch-on.

Still wearing my tweed jacket and tie from work, I met my then wife and her posh co-worker, entering the Town Hall at the back, then up a flight or two of stone steps. There was a balcony at the top, so of course, I stepped out onto it.

In the square below, a massive crowd had gathered. I heard someone shout

"Look, Barry Grant!"

The person was referring to me. I heard this a lot at the time, as I had the same curly dark hair, lanky frame and laconic expression as the actor Paul Usher, who played the character Barry Grant in the Channel 4 soap opera *Brookside*. I'd often been told I looked like Barry Grant, now I WAS Barry Grant. To my left on the balcony was the entertainer and ventriloquist Bob Carolgees, who'd made a career out of having funny bones and thin material, consisting of a fake Yorkshire Terrier dog on a fake arm. Bob smiled and gave the nod to fellow professional Paul Usher/ Barry Grant. On my right was actor and comedian Ted Robbins, holding a bottle of beer. He also nodded and gave a wink to "Barry."

"Nice to see you, lads," I said, and waved at the crowd, who waved back and cheered. It was a crteditable bit of diplomacy for Manchester to invite Scouse favourite Paul, and if by any remote chance you're reading this, thanks for the moment in the spotlight, Mr. Usher.

I did no more five-a-side at the school, but the year turned and it was almost Easter 1985, the end of the spring term. I always marvelled at the optimism of the British school year. The spring term begins in January, in the middle of winter, and ends just before Easter, when the weather is often still freezing cold. That year it was so cold that it was perfect for a game of staff v. fifth year football. (The now familiar numbering of school years hadn't yet happened, and secondary school ran from the first year to the upper sixth.) The concept of adults playing sports against children is now so alien that it seems unlikely that it ever happened. Back then, it was a good opportunity for the adults to show who was boss.

Langley School field was perched in the middle of what was once moorland, so the wind whipped across it with violent gusts. I got going with my "can't kick a ball down Havelock Street" skills. Just on half time, the head of PE, grey hair streaming in the gale, picked up the ball in defence and ran up the wing. He passed the ball to me, and as he did so, the wind changed direction. Not knowing what to do, I booted a long pass into the penalty area from the halfway line. The wind was now blowing towards the kids' goal, and it picked up the ball, blowing it fifty yards, narrowly over the crossbar. What was meant as a long ball had become what looked like a shot, and the onlookers cheered. It was almost a spectacular goal, but it wasn't. It was enough to impress the kids and fellow teachers though, thus kudos all round.

Just before the end of the summer term, another Scouse teacher and I took the school minibus into Manchester to visit the Chinese cultural centre. My fellow Liverpudlian also taught the lower ability students; I wonder why? Maybe we were type cast. As the kids got on the bus, the politically incorrect language filled the air. Our vehicle was a community vehicle, which the kids nicknamed "the Langley spaz bus", as it had a wheelchair lift for disabled passengers. I knew we were in for an interesting afternoon. As we approached Chinatown, one of the students, a lad called Peter, who was particularly challenged with social, behavioural and emotional difficulties, enquired loudly and in an extreme racist manner ,

"Where's the effing n***** then?"

I can't even write what else he said. When you live on one of Europe's most run down estates, racism is the refuge of the downtrodden. It's no excuse and almost everyone abhors it, but it explains what happened decades later with Brexit.

I liked that school, tough as it was, and forgot that it was a limited time gig. I was filling in for a teacher who'd gone on secondment for an entire school year to do her Masters. Different times. She was returning and I had to go, with the knowledge that the childrens' reading and maths ages had improved during my short tenure.

The postscript to my time in Langley was that Liverpool F.C. had missed out on the league and the cup that season, but were in the final of the European Cup. The Mancunian caretaker joked with me -

"You've won nowt this season!"

"We'll see. Tonight is the European Cup final. We're going to win."

It was the 29th May 1985, and the game was at the Heysel Stadium in Brussels. Tragically, it was one of the worst hours for Liverpool fans, and fans of the game everywhere, when 39 people were killed when a wall collapsed. Most of those who died were Juventus fans, with our fans mainly to blame. It resulted in English clubs being banned from European football competitions until 1990, with Liverpool F.C. banned until 1991.

This became a source of resentment for Everton fans, as they had a great team at the time, and they didn't get their chance at the European Cup. Some Blues took to cheering on Man. Utd. when they played

Liverpool, and these feelings lasted for years. L.F.C. fans would reply that we saved them from embarrassment, as that's what would have happened to them, but a tragedy was nothing to joke or feel resentment about. It took years to heal Liverpool's relationship with Juventus, and with Italy.

Chapter Four

Get thee back to Yorkshire, lad.

Considering I didn't have a job for September, we had a remarkably interesting time in the summer of 1985.

Lillian had decided that she, too, wanted to be a teacher, and applied to Bretton Hall College of Education, near Wakefield. Moving wasn't a problem, as we'd discovered that, if you were a council tenant, you could move to a council house anywhere in the country. This must have been part of the Tories' "get on your bike" policy of social mobility- literally move to where the jobs are. We could have gone to any town or city, perhaps joining the Scouse exodus to Bournemouth, a lovely place to be on the dole, as some discovered. Instead we applied for a council gaff in that lovely West Yorkshire town. I got myself on the supply teacher list for the local council, and, whilst we were waiting, went off for a jolly Eurorail trip around western Europe. I'm not sure where the money came from, but it was all inexpensive back then.

On reporting to the council offices in Castleford, I was told that we'd been allocated a flat on an estate in the mining town of Normanton. Not having a clue about the place, I went round and inspected it. Few places could have been as grim as Hathershaw, but this place put Netherly to shame for grimness. I went back and complained that I was a council "key worker" (still no permanent job, actually) and Lillian got on the phone with her pregnant-with-small-baby routine (still fictional.) We were immediately upgraded to a house on a better estate, with its own parking space and a view onto a common grassed area. There were trees still in leaf and not a burnt out car in sight. Better still, no packs of wild dogs. This was more like it. Who needed Bournemouth?

We got a friend to drive the van across the Pennines, I decorated the place (again) and Lillian started at the college. Pretty soon, I had a job for the remainder of the term at Castleford High School. I was put to work teaching a variety of subjects and inevitably I was given the whistle and told to referee boys' football, which I wholeheartedly did. The school field wasn't quite as windswept at the one in Rochdale,but it wasn't exactly warm, either. Goals would usually be decided by who had the wind at their backs, and who could kick the ball out of the mud, after it had stuck fast in the goalmouth. Like all school fields, it was permanent mud from November onwards. Many schools sold off their playing fields in the 90s because they were so short of funds. Some still have playing fields, but avoid using them in winter by having built astroturf pitches known as Multi Use Gym Areas, known ominously as " the MUGA pitch."

There were the usual assortment of PE teachers, mostly weathered and unchanged since the previous decade.

"Eh lad," said one of them, "you do know that these pitches are where they filmed *Kes?* Brian Glover once stood right 'ere." I'm not sure if he added "Eh by gum" on the end, but he definitely told me this. I believed him, having no way to check the information. I later learned that the whole film was shot in and around Barnsley, in South Yorkshire, not West Yorkshire, at a place called St. Helens School. At the time I glowed with pride to follow in the footsteps of Mr. Sugden, but I'd been had over by what we Scousers call "a woolyback". This refers to a person from outside Liverpool, who lives in a rural area, and may have sheep DNA mixed in with his or her genes. It's a case of Liverpudlian exceptionality, having more in common with Wales or Ireland than the rest of the north of England.

The term passed without much incident, and I managed to interview for, and get, a job in a special school for children with learning difficulties, just outside Castleford. I didn't think I'd done very well in the interview but was told later by other teachers it was due to being a man. It was a mainly female staff and the head wanted to keep a gender balance, so I fitted the bill. I had no idea how to do the job other than enthusiasm to do so, and to compound matters, I was to teach year 5 and 6 juniors. No training, no knowledge, no problem for me. That was my thoughts going into January 1986.

I tried my best, and found out that, to keep on the good side of the deputy head, Mrs. Hindley, all I had to do was produce dramatic and colourful displays using "sugar" paper and poster paints. Mrs. H. had a stash of what she referred to as "display cloths", bits of material in various shades, which she draped around the classroom to artistic effect. I worked closely with the teacher next door, Pam, another brilliant teacher who was wonderful with the children. She told me to order sets of books on any topic from the library service, free of charge, on a chosen theme for the half term. Once delivered, Mrs. H. would arrive with the cloths, making the drapes just right to stand the books on, all the better to teach the kids to read them. We all loved Mrs. H., although she didn't do much to facilitate learning other than check I'd done my weekly lesson plans, then she'd sail off to drape some more cloths. I use the nautical metaphor to describe our esteemed deputy leader's movements, as she delighted in telling the story of how a male former colleague had described her as "a battleship in full flow." She did resemble a ship's figurehead, with ample bosom and characteristic footsteps from her high heeled boots.

When I complained that the reading scheme we used for the juniors was out of date, Mrs. H. didn't listen.

"We decided democratically on the Crown scheme before you arrived."

"When was that, then?"

"Some years ago. But it's perfectly adequate."

Pam told me the Crown scheme had come in around 1980, but wasn't aging well. The subject matter was far too young for children in top juniors, although the difficulty level was about right. I lobbied for the brand new Oxford Reading Tree books, but was told no. A week or two later, I was told that the literacy advisor was coming round to check what was happening. I'd discovered a set of old Janet and John readers, the same ones I'd used at junior school in the 1960's. On the morning of the advisor's visit, I scattered the Janet and John books around the classroom.

Mrs. H. came in just before the boss lady from the council, and saw the J and J copies. These were thought of as outdated anathema at the time, even though they'd done great service for me and my friends in our inner city school. We didn't know anyone who lived like J and J, with a nice big house with a nice big garden containing a swing, but we supposed there were rich kids somewhere who had this life. Now, this was just not the done thing to give the books to council estate kids. Mrs. H, on seeing the old but beloved readers, looked like she was suffering a mild stroke. The proud bosom wilted a second before she pounced into action, gathering the Janet and Johns and stuffing them out of sight. She then assumed her posh, lah-de-dah voice for the bigwig, assuring her that our teaching methods were quite up to date.

"Yes," I added, "we've ordered the new Oxford Reading Tree books, haven't we Mrs. Hindley?"

"Oh, yes dear!" and to the advisor, "such an enthusiastic young teacher!"

As they left I got a death stare from over her shoulder. The Oxford Reading Tree books arrived soon after, but only for my class. Once they moved up, the kids were back on the Crown scheme. There was no continuity between classes, little record keeping and no one really cared, so long as there was some reading, writing and arithmetic going on. The children were safe and happy, there was regular exercise and generous school dinners. We provided them with clothes if they were in dire need, and every year we'd take the younger children on holiday to Wakefield's Outdoor Residential Centre in Hornsea. Opened in 1938 as Wakefield Seaside School, it was still providing holidays to school children up to 2007, and was similar in concept to Liverpool Education Committee's centre at Colomendy.

There was regular football on the school field each week, which I led, with boys from years 5 and 6 having chaotic kick arounds, whilst the girls stayed with Pam, doing sewing. We didn't force any boys to play and they were quite free to sew with the girls if they wished, but, being 1986, we didn't really ask the girls if they wanted to join in with the match. That's one way of putting it, but it was so basic that I concentrated on getting them all to kick in the same direction. Nowadays I'd be asked what I was teaching them, and at the time I'd have said "nothing", but they were learning foot / eye coordination and social skills. I recall jogging up and down in my "I ran the World" t-shirt, which I'd earned for running just under three miles around Sefton Park.

At some point during my tenure, someone had the bright idea of a staff v. pupils football match. The older teachers had seen me running about furiously, trying to herd the juniors, and decided that Scouser+football= second Maradona, which, as we know, was a mistake. The assorted teachers turned out, older men sporting their guts and one of the older ladies swishing a hockey stick about. I had no idea they were relying on me as their star player. Some of the year 11 lads, learning difficulties or not, were quite large and at least one could control a ball whilst rushing forwards in the manner of his rugby league hero. I busied myself at the back, trying to prevent us conceding a goal, whilst in midfield, the lady with the hockey stick got stuck in.

"OW! That hockey stick chuffin' hurts!" complained one of the lads. "What thee laikin at?" he demanded. Yorkshire dialect was still popular in the 80s, though I hear it has now, sadly, begun dying out.

I tried to be everywhere at once but it wasn't much good when most of our team couldn't run. Finally, the female teacher playing hockey rather than football, connected with her stick and it dribbled into the correct goal. It was 1-1 and we decided to leave it at that, celebrations all round. A fellow Scouse teacher (there was always one) a woman around 40 years old, commented-

"Huh! I thought all Scousers could play football."

Yeah, just like all Braziians look like Pele, I thought.

At Hornsea, the football sessions would be two or three times a day, to run energy off in the morning, then to occupy the kids before and after the evening meal. Everyone had a great time though it was tiring for the staff. For many of our students it was their only holiday, and when they got on the beach at Hornsea, the first time they'd seen the sea. On at least one occasion, a lad ran fully clothed into the waves, being so amazed at this thing he'd only ever heard about. Being at least a decade younger than the other teachers, I was happy to keep pace with the kids, but sometimes we'd have what Mrs. H. described as "The Munsters effect". This was after the American telly series popular in the 1960s, where the family were all monsters of one variety or another, but otherwise perfectly nice. If they tried to interact with normal people, they, the normals, would immediately run away. We had this effect because our children were quite large ten and eleven year olds, but with the mental capacity of much younger kids. If we took them to a playground, during our excursions from the Hornsea centre, they'd run straight for equipment designed for five and six year olds. The parents of the actual five and six year olds would then swoop in with horrified glares at us, take their children away and depart…leaving us to enjoy our sandwiches in peace whilst the pupils occupied themselves for half an hour, bouncing on wooden animals and little roundabouts that they dwarfed.

One weekend around this time, in spring 1986, Lillian and I went to visit some friends of hers in south London. The bloke was originally from Warrington, it turned out, and on the spur of the moment, we decided to go to the Chelsea v. Liverpool match at Stamford Bridge. I know, this is impossible to fathom nowadays, when tickets are purchased online and sold out weeks in advance, but at that time, you could still just walk up and squash onto the terraces. It was slightly concerning on the tube train when a lad my age asked me for the time. I knew the trick, ask a suspected Scouser for the time and if he answers in Liverpudlian, batter him. As I hadn't been living in the 'Pool for some time, I answered in a posh voice,

"Quarter past two, old chap." There was no further trouble on the train, but there was violence in the air.

We got into the away end and were directly behind the goal when Dalglish smashed in his shot, which turned out to be the only one, and won us the league. It was joy all round, except from the Chelsea fans. We, the away supporters, were left locked in the ground after the final whistle, and when we were allowed out, there was a solid wall of police all the way to the underground station. Cockneys were hanging out of pub windows, abusing us in pure Chas n' Dave style and I'm surprised glasses weren't thrown at us . At the tube, the police were herding us onto the northbound train to Euston, but we managed to cut off, straight onto a southbound train.

"When we get there, walk off and look straight ahead", said my mate, also named Martin. "There'll be Chelsea fans everywhere, looking for stray Scousers to beat up."

As the train stopped, I could see he was correct. We walked past the Cockney nut jobs without a second glance, and away unharmed.

By way of a postscript, many years later I told this tale to an old school friend who had also been at the match, and who went to make his own way home, as he was living in London as a student at the time. He was approached by two smartly dressed lads in suits, carrying brollies, when police dived on the besuited gents.

"Those weren't brollies, they were sword sticks, and they were about to draw them to use on you", he was told. I think I can say that the Met Police did OK that day.

With my new status as a permanent teacher and Lillian heading towards the end of her training, we could apply for a mortgage to buy a house.

We were both 26 and felt very grown up. I'd worked in a few different schools already, and Lillian landed a job in a mainstream junior school straight away, to start in September. We decided on a stone- fronted semi detached house in the town of Ossett, a bit further away from the school, although I'd just passed my driving test at the sixth attempt. The house was almost a hundred years old, with high ceilings and gloomy rooms, looking over a Victorian gothic graveyard next to a church. The price was £22000, which, in today's money, is £63,706, so you can see how affordable it was. The only other problem was some bad subsidence in the back of the property, which gave the unsettling effect of walking down hill to get to the kitchen. The back bedroom was similarly lopsided, but the owners said it had been underpinned and it was all OK. We got a quick survey done, which it passed, and were granted a 100% mortgage at 12%, which was all good as the purchase price was so low.

The house was somewhat odd, to the extent that some visitors declared it "haunted". A sideboard in the corner of the backroom would be perfectly fine all day, until we came in after work, and the door would swing open. Once, a mist emerged and dissipated into the air. I put this down to turning the central heating on, and the mist was just the cold air from inside the sideboard meeting warm air. During the evening, the door to the back room would move of its own volition. I put this down to draughty windows and the sloping floor. Our pet cat, which we'd acquired in Hathershaw when it turned up at our door one night, looking cute, would stare at invisible objects which fascinated it. At bedtime, upon turning out the lights, there'd be spooky noises, which I put down to the house "settling for the night" and the creaky heating system shutting down. There were even noises from above in the loft, which I never dared to enter. A year or so later, I realised some slates had dislodged from the roof and I got them fixed. The noises, no doubt made by birds that had got in, ceased immediately.

Lillian, in her inimitable way, decided to go to war with the church next to the gothic graveyard. It had a clock which chimed loudly every quarter hour. I'd just be finally drifting off when "BONG!BONG!" I'm not going to write out all the bongs, but it certainly let you know what time it was. Lillian put in a complaint to the council and they installed noise monitoring equipment. The vicar was informed and was not best pleased, but eventually the council decided the clock wasn't loud enough to constitute noise pollution, but that the bongs had to be turned off after 10 o'clock. We'd already made our mark in the small market town.

Our marriage wasn't great by this time and only got worse. It got to the point where we just ignored each other. Lillian had gone on a fad diet which she reckoned would cure her ills, but all it did was empty my bank account. Neither of us was easy to live with and so Lillian did the right thing and moved out, staying with friends in London and soon getting a job there, leaving me with the spooky house and the bongs. I was disappointed for a few days but went on holiday with my Scouse friends John (Smithy from school) and his mate Cranie, who he knew through supporting Everton. The holiday was notable because, being a proper Scouse scally, Cranie paid for the flight only and kipped on the floor, finally going home after one week rather than two, as he preferred fitting carpets in Breck Road to lying on beaches in Corfu.

This left me with a quandary- what to do. I paid off Lillian's share of the house and began catching up with old university friends who were

Yorkshire based. I realised that I was still young, and had a few years until I reached thirty to enjoy myself. I got into house and hip music and spent Friday and Saturday nights in Leeds, where a friend of a friend introduced me to Ricky's club, where two young DJs who called themselves "Nightmares on Wax" played all the latest tunes from Public Enemy, Eric B. and Rakim, Stetsasonic and British rapper Derek B. The big record of 1987 was Pump up the Volume by MARRS and we enjoyed this over and over again. I went to London at this time and visited the well known Wag Club, but it was tame compared to Ricky's. There was an upper dance floor where some particularly talented blokes danced to jazz, without making idiots of themselves. On the downstairs dancefloor, I was reliving my glory days of the Bali Hai.

Around this time, Liverpool F.C. got on the hip hop bandwagon by releasing their embarrassing *Anfield Rap* song. The team must have been so confident that they would win the 1988 F.A. cup final that they put their caps on backwards and mugged about for the camera, instead of getting on with practice. Everyone knew the match, against Wimbledon F.C. (who?) would be a mere formality…all Liverpool had to do was turn up. At the school, there was a jumble sale which Mrs. H. cajoled me into helping out with, so I promised to do the first hour and go home for the second half. By the time I turned on my state of the art Sanyo telly, (complete with four channels) Lawrie Sanchez had already scored , but I wasn't bothered. Peter Beardsley then had a goal ruled out before John Aldridge was fouled and we got a penalty. Right, this was it, score this then get the winner. Big Dave Beasant saved it and a few minutes later, Wimbledon had won the F.A. cup. I was struggling to take it in,to say the least, but now, I blame the *Anfield Rap* for the bad karma.

I'd enjoyed the night clubs in Leeds, but it couldn't last. I didn't want to be the oldest hip hopper in West Yorkshire and I knew that this scene would pass anyway, as punk rock had done. I didn't want to keep living in a house which was perfect to be investigated by Scooby Doo and his friends, and was freezing cold in winter. Although the job at the special school was lovely, after a few years I was growing bored.

I saw an advert in the Times Educational Supplement for the Fulbright Teacher Exchange Programme. I would go to a school somewhere in the United States for a year and the American teacher would reciprocate. Sounds great! I couldn't wait to do this, although the thought of "anywhere in the United States" might mean Nome, Alaska or Crapsville, Arizona did cross my mind. But what an adventure it would be! I'd always fancied the idea of moving to America since I got hooked on D.C. comics as a small kid. All I had to do to get by the one-year-only rule was to marry an American, then, problem solved! I'd rent out Spooky Mansions for the year then sell it.

I passed the interview and even met a Manc lad from the next market town over - his name was Roy and he lived in Horbury- who was also going on the same deal. We were both excited and couldn't wait. He invited me to turn out for his local football team and of course it didn't go too well, but I was surprised that, after the game, no one cared about the result and there was plenty of beer, a buffet and general bonhomie.

Whilst I counted down the months, I discovered that Wakefield council owned another hidden gem, Woolley Hall.It was a rather magnificent 17th century manor house, where those in the know could go for weekend courses, with free food (waitress service) and board. Long serving and well connected Wakefield education senior teachers got jobs as "advisors", and spent their working days in the lovely Woolley environment. Those were t' days, eh? One weekend I busied myself there, learning very little that would aid me in my teaching, but enjoying wine, beer and flirting. Somehow the flirting went a little too far and I embarked on a fling with a blonde junior school teacher, who just happened to be married. "Good", I thought, "I'm going to America, just what I need in the short term." I gave no thought to what would happen to her relationship with her husband or how he felt. I was having a good time- who cared?

The affair with my blond, Yorkshire married friend was short and passionate. I got to like her as a person; she had a personality and intellect that belied her "bimbo" looks. She told me some anecdotes that had been told to her by parents of kids she taught, on various parents' evenings.

"No one were more surprised than me when 'ee turned out to be Chinese," she said of her son. " His father were a soldier I met at Pontefract station one night when train were late. It were dark."

Our passion dragged on into the summer and I almost chose not to go to the United States after all. I even introduced her to my mum. Then I saw reason, and after one last romantic phone call at Heathrow airport, I never saw nor heard from her again.

We all know what happened towards the end of the 1989 football season. I was driving over to see my dad, who was living near Kirkby with his second wife. It was a surprisingly warm day for April and, as I got stuck in the customary traffic jam on the M62, news started coming in about Hillsborough. It was all confused and confusing at first, but by the time I got to my dad's, the scale of it was beginning to be known. It was made worse when I spoke to my mum the next day; she worked on the switchboard at Alder Hey childrens' hospital, and in the lack of coordination at the time, no special hotline had been set up. It was left to my mum to answer calls from parents trying to find their kids, and a lot of Hillsborough victims were children. In ways like this, thousands of Scousers were affected by the tragedy.

The best outcome to the '89 final was when Liverpool beat Everton after a fantastic 3-2 game. The Toffees did their best to win and that added to the excitement. Whichever team had won, the trophy would have come to the city, but it was the right result. Our family gathered again outside our house, on the same spot where Shankly had applauded our house decorations in 1973. As the bus passed, I raised my fist in solidarity for the team, meaning "you did it for the Hillsborough fans." Steve Nichol, knowing exactly what I meant, gave me the one fisted salute right back.

Liverpool was also certain to win the league the next weekend, securing the double. All they had to do was not lose more than one nil to Arsenal at home. Just get a draw at Anfield, win the double! Of course it was nailed on, as the 1988 cup final had been. I went for a few bevvies with Roy in Wakefield, having taped the match to enjoy later. Getting on the bus, I heard a few Woolybacks muttering that Arsenal had won. What? I questioned one of them.

"Aye, Arsenal won two nil and won the bloody league!"

Arsenal had done it again! The same team that broke my heart in 1971. That was two Arsenal players on my target list- Charlie George and Michael Thomas. Liverpool had their own way of dealing with Thomas, however. They bought him, only for him to play but few decent games ever again. He did score in the '92 FA cup final, but apart from that, he was mostly injured.

Chapter Five

Not Born in America

Although I'd fancied moving to the States for many years, I found myself very isolated. After a first week of induction at Georgetown University in Washington D.C., I was posted to the small town of Lewes, Delaware. Virtually nothing seemed to happen there (although there were things going on, hidden just below the surface.)

There was an ice cream shop, a pub , a library and the beach, so it wasn't all bad, but I felt completely uprooted, which I was. I borrowed Robinson Crusoe from the library and read the whole thing, feeling just like him, although, of course, there were many people around. The internet, still not having been invented, the nearest I got to home was a short-wave radio purchased from Radio Shack at one of the roadside strip malls. The signal drifted in and out at night, except for one Saturday afternoon I got a great signal from Anfield, via the World Service, with live commentary on the match.

I went up to D.C. to visit Roy, who was staying with a teacher from the school he'd been assigned to, Mary. She had a terraced house only a few streets from the White House, but it was surprising how quickly the neighbourhoods changed in D.C. When it was my turn to buy beer from the corner shop, I noticed three men standing around outside, having a laugh and a joke. They didn't bother me, I didn't bother them.

"Who are those blokes outside the shop?" I asked Mary, somewhat naively.

"Oh, don't worry about them, they're fine." she said. Just yer friendly neighbourhood drug dealers.

Next day, Roy decided to do his laundry and dry it, causing Mary's dryer to overheat and cut out.

"Oh, I've fucked it up, it's fuckin broke" he panicked, in broad Manc.

"Leave it to reset, Roy. It's cut out. In the meantime, we'll find a launderette to dry your stuff."

The nearest one in the Yellow Pages was pinpointed to P street, a couple of blocks away. Again, the neighbourhood changed, and we were the only white people in sight, which I didn't consider a problem. Then I noticed an African American bloke turn to look at us- two tall white men in a black neighbourhood, wearing shades and carrying a holdall were, looking back on the situation, a cause for suspicion. Perhaps everyone breathed easy when we turned in at the door of the launderette.

Back in Lewes, things improved as term began and I met some other teachers my age. I heard that there was a football (soccer) session over at the middle school, so I went over to help. The coach was a smooth spoken Yank in his mid thirties, with sand coloured hair and a goatee beard. I recall him referring to one of the boys as "Golden", and I couldn't work out if this was the lad's first name, surname or nickname. The lad seemed confused too, but not as confused as I was when the coach passed me the ball, only for me to mistime it and miss my kick completely.

"Bad bounce," he said in consolation. Totally ashamed, I never went back to the middle school soccer practice again that year.

Instead, I concentrated on my project of marrying an American, so I could stay. It's difficult to fathom why I was still on this quest, having hated the isolation of the first few weeks, but I do like a mission to give myself a purpose. I met a beautiful girl from Delaware itself, called Janis. She was an ideal height at 5 foot seven, with long brown hair and large eyes the same colour. Janis' head was round and pretty, and although she joked that she had a "pumpkinhead" she looked just great. Her olive skin tanned to a fashionable light brown in summer, and in 1990 Janis was the most beautiful girl on Rehoboth Beach.

Janis worked at an elementary school but coached the high school cheerleaders. She explained the cheerleading hierarchy to me; prettiest and most athletic girls cheered for football, whilst the homeliest cheered for the strictly redneck sport of wrestling. Of course, Janis coached the football cheerleaders. I could forgive some of her right wing views as her dad had been in the U.S. air force, flying regularly from Dover, Delaware to Burtonwood, near Warrington. I thought this was a great thing to have as a link with Janis- her dad was almost an honorary Scouser.

There's a lot to tell about the school year of 1989-1990 in lower, slower Delaware, but little of it has to do with football. One weekend, I met up with Roy and his girlfriend Dinah, up in New York City. It was becoming cold in November 1989; every channel on the telly in the hotel was showing porn, so I went for a ride to the top of the Empire State building. I spoke to a bloke from West Germany-

"The Berlin Wall is coming down," I stated rather obviously, even though in the American news hierarchy, it had been the second in importance, behind a boating accident in Pennsylvania.

The German bloke looked out over the famous view, the subject of thousands of tourist photos, and stated that it was momentous, and where he was living, this epoch defining event had also been reported as a lesser item behind some local trivia.

"Do you think West Germany will ever reunify with the East?" I asked.

"No, no, that will never happen. The East is too vast and too poor." Seeing into the future is difficult, even from the top of the Empire State.

The same evening, I met up with Roy and his girlfriend Diane, who'd come to live with him for the remainder of the year. Our aim was to reach the twin towers of the World Trade Center and see the cityscape lit up at night. We must have got off the subway (which was quite an experience in 1989) a stop or two early, as we found ourselves in the deserted business district, which was completely silent at that hour. Roy saw a short cut down a street called Bowery. I was well aware of the street's reputation as a dangerous area inhabited by homeless and alcoholics, and I told Roy this.

"Nah, it'll be ok", was his optimistic opinion.

About half way along Bowery the silence became pervasive. Traffic could be heard from afar, but there was none on this street. All the Batman comics featuring the danger of Gotham City came to mind, and although I didn't expect The Joker to appear, it was exactly his kind of territory. From nowhere, a milk bottle smashed onto the pavement three feet in front of us. To me, it seemed like it had been chucked from several floors up in one of the buildings, but Roy now maintains it was thrown from a car. Nevertheless, we were used to the shitholes of Liverpool and Manchester; it gave me a fright for thirty seconds, but we kept on walking, our pace a little faster.

New York City in 1989 had begun the process of gentrification but you only had to go to the west side of midtown Manhattan to see areas that still looked like derelict Liverpool docks. I could understand why John Lennon had loved the place- it was Scouseland on steroids, with an attitude. I'd enjoyed finding the original American F.W. Woolworth's store, as our U.K. original on Church Street had been replaced by a British imitation with a different logo. The experience came complete with some verbal abuse from a shop assistant, which I loved; the true NYC experience. Now, the city is nothing like Liverpool- it's a generic metropolis like London or Shanghai, with many of the same globalised shops and cafes. I'm sure there's still crime in New York City, but it feels much safer; even the subway, where much of the action took place in 1979 gang film *The Warriors*, feels safe and nowadays, if you cross 110th street, as Bobby Womack famously sang about, it's just another quiet uptown neighbourhood.

Back in lower Delaware and needing a vehicle, eventually I purchased a knackered Jeep, which I loved as it was a quintessential bit of Americana- except it had little or nothing in the way of brakes, and the wings, or fenders, were rusted through. Some duct tape and a can of yellow paint sorted that out. I moved to a better flat In Rehoboth and, when my mum asked me if there was anything she could send, I requested a copy of the Football Echo, which arrived surprisingly quickly, four days later. I discovered that the landlord and landlady of The Old Campfield on Hayworth Street were doing well, and sent greetings to all customers for the upcoming holiday season. My relationship with Janis was going great; she drank heavily, but so did I, and when I realised she was neurotic I thought, so was Lillian, and at least this one is pretty. By the time I had to go back to the U.K. we'd decided we were soul mates and would get engaged in the autumn. This was my masterplan- I had to go back to Yorkshire for at least a term as part of my programme, but, by coming over in October and putting a big diamond on Janis' finger, I'd claim her as mine. I'd learned nothing from my university relationship with Gill ten years earlier, where I found out that women have minds of their own, and not even a large, shiny jewel would do the trick if I was 3000 miles away most of the time. Heck, it hadn't even worked out with Gill when I was less than 3000 yards away.

I ended the year out in Colorado where I'd driven with my roommate and some of his friends, listening to the 1990 world cup on the short wave while we drove. I could just about make out the dramatic England v. Cameroon match through the static. None of the Yanks were even remotely interested, of course. After some interesting driving including an unscheduled turnoff in Kansas whilst I was at the wheel as the Americans slept, they left me in a hotel where I checked in to watch the semi final versus Germany. It was the fourth of July and I was the only hotel guest whilst everyone else was out celebrating. The match was another thriller with the only outcome possible- we lost to Germany (or West Germany, at the time) on penalties. Later, a couple of smart arse Yanks made wise cracks-

"Fourth of July was never a great day for the English, eh, buddy?" I tried to think of a witty comeback but decided "fuck off Yank" might not have gone down too well in a bar full of them. Decades later I came up with the genius reply that, if they'd been in Colorado in 1776, they'd have been raped, scalped and murdered by the Cheyanne and Shoshone tribes. Again, this might not have elicited a great response at the time.

The lack of any internet (it had been invented but hadn't yet reached the masses, only reaching 16 million users by 1995) meant that a friend now had to drive me to the airport in Denver to get my ticket for the first part of the journey home, and on the way we were caught in a storm with hail the size and weight of golf balls, the occasional one reaching the size of a baseball. His car was battered and the windscreen smashed. I'd never encountered weather like that before, nor have I encountered it since. From Colorado I got a flight to San Francisco, and after "hanging out with all the boys" at the YMCA for a few days ,(it was the cheapest accommodation available) I flew home to London, then Liverpool. When I arrived back at my mum's house, I found out that Liverpool F.C. had won the championship with two games to spare. We were back at the top again, and surely that's where we'd stay throughout the 1990s. I'd totally missed the poll tax riots but happily, I was back in time to see Thatcher leave Downing Street in tears that November.

I got Spooky Mansions back from the tenants in September, and spent the weekend cleaning it. They'd been heavy smokers, but perhaps this had driven the ghosts away, as I had no more trouble; or perhaps it was because I'd had the roof mended. I put it on the market and it sold in a month- I'd be off back to the States in the new year. Janis came and stayed there at Christmas and cut an incongruous figure in Yorkshire, as most Yanks do in England. She was as much fun as ever, although I had to buy extra booze on many occasions. All autumn, I'd been phoning the U.S. Embassy to sort out my fiance's visa, but with no luck. Phones were still the old, heavy rotary style, yet I'd mastered the art of dialling in the number super fast; still, it was permanently engaged.

Having resigned in Yorkshire I got a job for one term in a junior school in Maghull, near Liverpool. I organised a football match with another local junior side, and as we were only a one form entry, it was a struggle to get eleven players and a couple of subs. One lad I chose was a typical nerd who could hardly kick a ball; I thought of my own delight at playing for the juniors B team. Another male teacher at the school watched the lad as he pulled on his shin pads and said-

"He'll always remember the time he played for the school team". Who cared what the score was- in my one term I brought a little joy to the school and it was a pleasure to teach some children who, I had to admit, were brighter than I was. This was a first, and a pleasure to have helped them on their way. I hope they all grew up to be neuro- surgeons, top barristers and even, humble but talented teachers.

At Easter Janis and I skied in Colorado, courtesy of air tickets from her parents, and already things weren't great. We were trying to make a go of it, but her drinking had reached a level where Janis kept a flask of vodka or Jagermeister permanently around her neck. Setting off on a ski run, she crashed into me and knocked me over. Perhaps this may sound like the most middle class reason to end a relationship and Breckenridge, Colorado was a long way from Haverlock Street, but I was losing patience. By the summer, knowing quite well that my two carat diamond hadn't prevented Janis from straying, it was over, but not before one last night where we drank a lot of beer and Janis attempted a cartwheel in cheerleader style, to see if she still "had it." Janis certainly did, as the mosquitos circled and the cicadas choroused around the August barbeque. Janis was quite some girl. The previous summer, we'd been drinking in a local bar when she met the owner of a 30 foot yacht, a woman Janis vaguely knew, who resembled Brunhilda of Valkyries fame. The Norse looking seafarer had steered her vessel up from Florida for the summer and asked if we wanted to go for a ride. Janis and I were both quite drunk, so of course we both said "yes".

Next thing, I was off down the Lewes and Rehoboth canal and out onto the Roosevelt Inlet, then almost onto the Atlantic.

"Hey, you wanna steer?" asked Brunhilde, her blonde plaits swinging behind her deeply suntanned face.

"Certainly," I said. Which Scouser doesn't want to steer a 30 foot yacht when drunk? I'm sure many of my fellow Liverpudlians navigated the westward passage on sailing ships, half cut.

"Just head in between those two lights," said the skipper.

"THIS IS THE U.S. COAST GUARD!" A motor cruiser had pulled up some distance away and was on the loudspeaker.

"What are you doing out here at this time of night?" They politely enquired.

"Just fishin'", said our captain, and held up a fish, caught earlier, that she was in the process of gutting.

"Take her in. You can't be out here in the hours of darkness!" the coast guard commanded us.

We turned around and went back in, with fresh fish to cook, which we barbecued on a disposable grill. We had driven a short distance to the boat in the knackered jeep, and turning on the radio, I got Sinatra on a distant, crackly station.

Having split up with Janis, I didn't want to let her win by denying me my right to live in the United States. That had been my goal- meet a beautiful American lady, marry her and live happily ever after in the suburbs. As Janis herself had pointed out, that was "some fuckin' *Leave it to Beaver* fantasy," quoting the name of a still popular television show of the 1950s. Of course, she was right, but I wouldn't accept it- like the Monty Python goalkeepers, I was a dreamer, a romantic. I'd spent the early part of the summer writing to school districts applying for a job, with no success and few replies. Now, I was over on holiday to see my remaining friends,before I gave up completely on the United States. It was time for one last chance to get a job without having to rely on citizenship gained via the marriage route. I called the office at Indian River School district, the next one down the peninsula from where I'd been the year before, with no great expectation. Thanks to some help from Janis' mum, I had all my certification to teach in the state of Delaware. I got through to the switchboard relatively easily, after some small delay, to the head honcho.

"What do you teach?" he asked. I explained…special needs, special education, English.

"Can ya come in for an interview tomorrow and do ya have I.D?"

I asked what he needed. As well as the certification to teach in state, I had a social security number and a driving licence, which was all that was needed. By some tremendous coincidence, Indian River High School was short of a special education teacher, as the lady from the previous year didn't have the correct Delaware qualification, which I did. I explained that I didn't have a work visa.

"No problem, Mack, we'll sort all that out for ya."

I got a lift into the office the next day with Scott, my friend from Colorado, who'd fixed, filled and flatted his Volkswagen Scirocco and had it painted back to its original white, after the hailstone incident the year before. The job was mine and I started next week. No problem that I'd only come over on holiday and had just one suitcase of clothes. As I was leaving, the district superintendent said-

"By the way, Mack, they need an assistant soccer coach at the high school. That something ya can do? It comes with some pay, not much but extra on ya salary". Perhaps he called me Martin, perhaps he didn't talk like Tony Soprano, but that was the gist of it.

"Sure," I said,"right up my street."

A day or two later I was in a country diner which could only have existed in the back roads of America, with the principal, Dr. Patterson, and the athletic director, a squat grey haired man who looked the antithesis of athletic.

The walls were clad in a type of plastic laminate that my dad had used in our kitchen when we'd first moved to the council house in 1972 and which we'd found out, after an unfortunate chip pan fire, that said laminate was flammable. My dad, braving the smoke, had put out the flames, then retired to the garden to clear his lungs by smoking a cigarette. The athletic director was wearing another 1970s throwback, a loud brown and yellow checked jacket that I'd bought the replica of in 1975, after my mum had given me some money and trusted me to go shopping on my own in town, to purchase some appropriate gear for a cousin's wedding. I'd paired this abomination with a pair of grey flared slacks, and I noticed that the athletic director had done the same, but his slacks were yellow. If someone had been asked to draw a caricature of a typical loud Yank, it was this guy. By contrast, Dr. Patterson, although not exactly dressed up, looked the height of sartorial elegance.

"So, is it Martin, or Mack?" asked the man in the ridiculous attire.

"Martin is fine."

"That's an American name, but I hear ya British. You'll sure be an expert on soccer then?" I confirmed that yes, I was an expert as I came from Liverpool.

"Well, we're just developing our soccer program over here but you sure will be a great addition to the team." He shook my hand. "Congratulations, Mack. Martha, more coffee over here please, honey". More of America's favourite, the stuff that sits on one of those machines and evaporates all day into a black syrup, was poured all round. The thought occurred that I was now going to be paid to coach football, which surely made me a professional.

I rented a unit in a swanky development in Bethany Beach, which, now that the summer was over, became a lot cheaper during the autumn and winter seasons. September was still very warm, and football (soccer) practice began. To start with, I was kicking balls back as the lads took shots, but soon I got to know them and I was sharing small group training with Head Coach, Phil Mead. I began to advise Phil on who to select for the team, devising training methods, working with the goalies, practising "the long throw" (no offside from a throw in, I told them), and generally getting the team ready for our first game. We had a great centre forward, a tall Spanish exchange student at centre half and a lad who was more built for American football in the centre of defence, called Brian. Phil said that he wanted "a strong spine" to the team, and I agreed. We began well with a win, then played a team of skinheads from Milton District High School. Their coach was also British and had told all his lads to get crew cut haircuts to look like 1970s football hooligans. My advice to our lads was "Get stuck in!"

I told them that, "This bunch think they're hard, let's show them what's what!" It became a somewhat bloody encounter, with cut legs and scraped heads, and ended in a 2-2 draw and a few players hobbling off. But at least they knew that Indian River took no prisoners.

As the season drew on, we played under floodlights. Every American sports ground has floodlights as High School American football is a big deal, especially out in the sticks where there are no professional teams. We had bleachers on either side of the pitch, but some schools had proper stadiums, I was told, the richer schools upstate. The standard of refereeing was very poor as many of the refs hardly understood the rules, and were moonlighting from their regular gigs as American football refs. After one brightly floodlit game, as the players and officials walked off, I had a word with the ref.

"Thank you for the best refereeing I have seen since I have been over here. You really know the game."

"Och, thanks very much," said the Scots guy. There were quite a few of us Brits in the area, it seemed.

Another time, we sized up our opposition team, which boasted a couple of Mexican lads. One of them had the low centre of gravity and surly looks of Maradona, and was playing a game of keepie uppie on his own...I didn't give much for our chances. Greg, our centre forward, kicked off and passed it back to Spanish exchange student Carlos, who claimed to be eighteen but looked twenty seven. Carlos charged straight through, passed it to Greg and he scored. At the half time whistle, we were five-nil up. Phil gave his team talk and I gave mine-

"Whatever you do, don't sit back on this lead- it could still go either way. Keep the pressure on them, keep the ball and keep attacking. Be solid at the back."

After 90 minutes, it was still five nil. So much for Maradona and his mates.

I almost felt revenge for the "hand of God" incident in 1986.

At the end of the regular season, Phil announced that we'd done so well that we were one of the top teams in the state and therefore qualified for the state tournament on a knockout basis. I had no idea there was such a thing as the state tournament, but this was exciting stuff! Delaware was the second smallest state in the U.S., but we were one of the sixteen best high school teams in it. This was light years from dodging dog shit in the park.

The first game, in the round of sixteen, was at Caesar Rodney High School. This is a massive school, upstate in Kent County. It is well known and has much better facilities. Janis had gone to this school as Dover Air Force base is in the catchment area. The stadium is called Rider Stadium, and looks like a place where international athletics could take place- in 1991, it reminded me of Crystal Palace athletics stadium, which was then still thriving. As darkness came down and the stadium was floodlit, it was almost- but not quite- like being at Anfield, but as a manager. I imagined leading out my team, at night, at a lower league stadium- perhaps Boundary Park, Oldham- and even though this upmarket high school soccer pitch wasn't the heights of the first division, it was probably as near as I'd ever get.

We kicked off, Phil and I secretly without a great deal of hope against our bigger and better financed opponents. To the players, we'd enthused about our chances, and had carefully explained our game plan. Greg and Carlos, our two stars, were in top form, and other lads seemed to have visibly grown during the season. During the first half our goalkeeper was injured and we brought him off to replace him with our second string keeper, a young man who would get crippled with nerves if we told him he was playing, but who had the physical strength to throw the ball to the halfway line. He had no time for nerves- he was straight on, and there was a gasp from the four hundred strong crowd as he chucked the ball from his area at the first opportunity, straight into the path of our best lads. Greg scored and I could hear his dad going mental from the bleachers; we were one up.

The match ended four- two; we'd completed the greatest giant killing act since Hereford United beat Newcastle 2-1 in the 1972 F.A. Cup. The Caesar Rodney Riders, named after an eighteenth century Delaware founding father, were dejected. This was genuinely unexpected; Phil and I ran on to congratulate the lads, who were celebrating this famous victory. It was as good as winning the whole tournament for us, and the yellow school bus back to Frankford would have been full of popping champagne corks, if only they'd been old enough to drink. We stopped at a McDonalds instead. I hardly remember the quarter final, although we were well beaten in it- we'd had our glorious sunshine moment.

The local paper had done a write up about our team, declaring that "assistant varsity coach and Liverpool, England native Martin MaCarrol (sic) owns a solid soccer background". If you can call a career playing in the junior school B team and the secondary school All Stars a "solid soccer background" then yes, I was a genius. To cap the season off, the parents association, or, in American parlance, the "I.R Soccer Boosters" presented me with an embroidered "Coach Mack" button- up nylon sports jacket, a "Coach Mack" hoodie and a long sleeved green polo shirt, with the full title "Coach Mackarel." I was so taken with the jacket that I paid for another one to send to my dad, who'd just survived an aortic aneurysm that should normally have killed him, at the relatively young age of fifty six. When he eventually received it, he loved the jacket and said he wore it when he "wanted to look 'ard", like the lads with the crew cuts from Milton High School. As a coincidence to all this, I was at home at Christmas at my mum's watching *Blue Peter* with Nick- we were both grown adults by now and I was past thirty, but we'd grown up with the show- when the Caesar Rodney school marching band came on.

"We beat them at football!" I shouted. "Nick, we battered this lot!"

Nick couldn't quite gather how his brother had beaten up an American high school marching band, but nevertheless, it was a reminder of my achievement with the great Indian River "soccer" team of autumn 1991.

When I returned, the remainder of the school year was spent being busy at the school, and with my new girlfriend, Lynda. She was a newly qualified teacher and nine years younger than me at a mere twenty two. Lynda was shorter but cuter than Janis, and from Illinois in the midwest. She made me think of the Beach Boys song *California Girls*

"The midwest farmer's daughters really make you feel alright." Even though her dad was a bank manager, she fitted the bill, with her youthful, wholesome, American-as apple-pie looks. In addition, she was permanently cheerful; like the character Pollyanna, Lynda was ceaselessly optimistic, in contrast to my less then happy morning demeanour. We took turns driving to work and I tried to forget about the tempestuous Janis, with whom I'd had a roller coaster ride of a relationship so recently.

I made sure to tell Lynda that, due to my visa situation, I'd probably have to leave at the end of the school year, as the Head Honco at the school district was having no luck in that direction. She was ok with that as, at twenty two, she had no intentions of settling down yet, and thought I was a little too old for her in any case. This didn't hinder our relationship in any way. The apartment would have to go too, towards the end of the school year, as the lucrative summer rental market would begin again for the owner, Don. Lynda and I settled into a passionate, comfortable,but, we agreed, temporary relationship.

During the winter there was no football (soccer) so I volunteered to accompany the junior varsity basketball team to their match against Cape Henlopen, which was the school district where I'd worked on my exchange year. There was one particular lad called Nathan, whom his team mates had christened "Nate the Great". He was only about five foot nine in height, but as soon as he got the ball, he would avoid the Cape Henlopen defenders and dunk it. He kept doing this, and they had no response. At half time, my Indian River team was miles ahead. The boys gathered for the coach's team talk.

"Look, lads" I said, "I don't know a lot about basketball, but whatever you're doing, keep doing it, as it's going great."

"Right, coach," they replied, went out and ran up the score even more. It was very satisfying to beat our local rivals, Cape Henlopen, another High School that was much better funded than our own.

On 9th May, Liverpool won the F.A. cup for the fifth time, as I listened in on the World Service. Ian Rush scored the other goal (as previously mentioned, our import from Arsenal, Michael Thomas, had scored the first.) The Reds had a lucky route to victory, having struggled to beat Portsmouth in the semi, and faced a Second Division team, Sunderland, in the final. It was the closing months before the Premier League began, and L.F.C. only managed sixth place in their last First Division season. Things weren't going as well as expected, but they'd won a trophy; who knew it was to be one of only two major prizes the club gained in the 1990s?

My final day at Indian River came along. There was no work visa for me and the original teacher from the previous year was coming back. It was another situation like seven years earlier at Langley- I liked the job, the students and the teachers, but I had to go. My colleagues and I needed to have our planning books signed off by the principal, Dr. Patterson, before we could leave for the summer. As he checked and signed my book, I thought back to an early morning earlier in the year, when I'd visited the men's staff toilets. I'd seen that there were the usual urinals and one toilet cubicle, but there was another toilet in the middle of the floor. In a story by an American writer, I'd discovered that Yank men thought it "manly" to have a shit in the open, where they could be beheld by their brothers in defecation. Never did I think I'd see another bloke use the visible bog, but that day, there was Dr. Patterson, pants around his ankles, taking his time with his daily bowel movement.

"Mornin' Mr. Mackarel", he greeted me.

"Mornin' Dr. Patterson", I replied, used the non-visible toilet in the stall and left as soon as possible.

Other teachers had once told me-

"If you're nervous at being interviewed by the head teacher for a job, just imagine them taking a shit."

I no longer had to imagine it. I could never forget it.

Back home yet again, I had a flat in Aigburth to move into. I'd seen it the previous summer and had conducted all the paperwork via fax from Frankford, Delaware. Fax technology had been invented in 1846 and had been in modern use since 1964, but I'd discovered it in 1991. Uncle Bill had helped me once again by renting out the flat in my absence, so almost immediately I once more had a place in the U.K. . My dad was no longer up to carrying gas stoves, but managed to get up the stairs and supervised whilst I assembled furniture. I went to see Ringo Starr and his All Star Band at the Liverpool Empire at the beginning of June, almost immediately upon returning, and noticed that the Scouse blokes' uniform hadn't changed; as I walked down Lime Street, every fella wore a shell suit, teamed with a curly perm and a moustache. It was the model for every Scouser skit for years afterwards.

A job was also easy to come by, and I started straight away at a school for students with learning difficulties in Huyton. I was thrown into P.E. again and had once or two decent footballers, although the head of P.E., a diminutive moustachioed man called Derek, wasn't to my liking. I was told that the job would be renewed for the autumn term, so I was well set again, and should have forgotten all about Lynda, as we'd agreed. These things never go to plan, though, and our relationship lingered. She moved to Atlanta, not having been retained at Indian

River and I visited in October. My dad took me to the airport in his new toy, a pale yellow 1979 Rolls Royce Silver Shadow. It was a beautiful car which frequently broke down, but this time, we got there ok.

"I'll never cease to be amazed by the lengths fellas will go to for a shag," he laughed.

"We're in luv!" I argued back. It was another one of those father/ son moments.

"Oh aye," he replied, "is that what they call it?

I finished at the school in Huyton that December and would start at Ruffwood School, Kirkby, in January.

Chapter Six

Frankly, my dear, I'd rather be in Kirkby.

January 1993 was the same as every other January in Kirkby- cold. I discovered that one of the coldest places on earth, other than the polar regions, was Ruffwood School playing fields. The winds seemed to rip across it more relentlessly than the corresponding moor top playing fields in Langley, but then, I'd been sensible enough to mainly play football indoors in Rochdale.

I'd been daft enough to immediately volunteer to manage the Year 9 football team, which I thought to be a good idea as it would get me out of bed on a Saturday morning. Sometimes I regretted it when I got heckled from the sidelines by the odd dad or grandad who turned up to watch; it was the custom for the teacher from the home team to referee the game. One bloke was giving me such aggro that I walked over and offered him the whistle.

"No lad, yer alright, me legs 'ave gone."

The particular match was quiet after that and the lads toiled on in the mud. It was the second half of their season and they appreciated now having a manager so much that they won most of their games. It was a happy time.

One morning in February, a television camera crew turned up at the game. Wandering over, I discovered that they were German, looking for a negative story about Merseyside in the wake of the James Bulger murder. Anyone who doesn't know what happened can look it up, but it was another knock back for all of us in the area, less than four years after Hillsborough.

"I am surprised to see the boys playing football on a Saturday," said the German news reporter.

"Yes, we are a very positive community around here. Things are improving." Someone had probably told them that, if you want to find a shit hole to report on, go to Kirkby.

"Our area is no worse than many regions in your own country," I added.

"Yes, certainly in the east", he agreed. In other words, we looked like a post Soviet landscape, complete with the featureless tower blocks. They walked off without filming. They hadn't found the required grimness, and I'd stood up for Kirkby, which, at the time, needed as many people as possible to stand up for it.

My team's most memorable match came one morning in early spring. Dave, the esteemed head of P.E., had told me that the lads' kit would be left in the changing rooms ready for our massive local derby against local school, All Saints. He'd given me the keys on Friday night and I turned up in good time to let the boys in. Mr. Murphy, headteacher of All Saints and year 9 manager arrived, with his team all ready and quickly changed into their kits. But where was our kit? I looked everywhere- no kit. I searched everywhere again- still no kit.

"Are your lads ready yet?" asked Mr Murphy. I explained the situation and he offered some spare shorts and, together with dirty shirts we found thrown into the showers and lost property, we cobbled together the best in the way of a "kit" we could manage. One lad had no socks but had shin pads, whilst another had a yellow bib to denote the same colour as our kit. We looked a right state as we walked out, with the All Saints team sniggering and some laughing out loud.

This must have fired up my boys, as they played the best I'd ever seen. In the words of current football pundits, they had "half a yard on the other team". It was still a close match though, and with five minutes to go of the hour- we played 30 minutes each way- the ball came to one of our least talented players, a lad who'd never scored. The ball bounced in front of him and he hit it on the volley, hitting the upper left hand side of the goal, which the thirteen year old goalie had no chance of stopping. Our scorer- the lad with only shin pads and no socks- thought he'd scored the winner in the F.A. cup final. He may as well have, as all these lads were local and knew each other. The goal was the winner and Ruffwood had "edged it in a tense local derby", as the report in the Football Echo might have run, if there'd been anyone there to record the match in print. There wasn't, so the game only exists in the minds of me, a despondent Mr. Murphy and the lads who played that day in 1993.

Managing the year 9 team wasn't the only footballing delight of early 1993. Ruffwood had its own teachers' football team; as a large comprehensive, we had enough male teachers young enough to field eleven a side, every week, against other local teachers' teams. In January and February, we played in the wilderness of the astroturf pitches in Skelmersdale. Currently, Skelmersdale has the JMO sports park, which doesn't resemble what existed over thirty years ago. At the time, it was a kind of rough green carpet with added sand for good measure, which, if you fell on it, gave you a nice road rash. With no give in the pitch, balls would bounce high into the floodlit night sky. I could never get the hang of predicting where they would land, and always misjudged the headers by approximately a yard. Our opposition were no better, and we'd go up to challenge for the ball, only to find that we'd both missed it. The wind would once more play a deciding factor in the matches, but we did have some very good players, as it turned out. I wasn't one of them, but Dave and the other young P.E. teacher could both play, as could the head of science and the French teacher. We also had a drama teacher, Little Frank, who was brilliant at going down for free kicks when he hadn't been touched. I think it was Frank who originated the custom of beating the ground whilst rolling in agony, only to jump up perfectly fine minutes later, a technique which is almost universally employed by Premier League players in the present day. Frank's theatrical antics once went on so long that we had to stop the game whilst he acted out his Shakespearean ambitions. Getting more than a little pissed off, Dave walked over to Frank and, without breaking stride, stood on the latter's leg with his full weight, giving him something to actually complain about. As Frank went into paroxysms of agony, Dave said

"Oh, sorry Frank, didn't see you down there."

Over a few bevvies later on, Frank liked to perform his party piece, the song "The Little Boy Who Santa Claus Forgot".

After half term, we could play in daylight once more, travelling to school pitches throughout Knowsley and Liverpool. At Cardinal Allen school in West Derby (now Cardinal Heenan) I found myself almost on the goal line ready for an in- swinging corner. Marked by a defender, I went up for the header and completely missed, as did he. The goalie was equally confused and had lost sight of the ball when it fell on my foot and bounced in. Of course, I had meant it all along and had deceived both goalie and defender.

With a pleasant flat in Aigburth, a job I liked and a gang of mates at the school, anyone would think I'd forget all about returning to the States, but not this lad. I'd decided that my future still lay across the Atlantic, and that I'd try to work it out with Lynda. I tried to get a job near her in Atlanta, but only got a reply from a school in Raleigh, North Carolina, who were keen to interview me. I said I'd be there during the middle of February and got on with sorting out my visa- I wasn't going to be defeated on that count, this time. I paid $3000 to a southern lawyer, who probably thought it was the easiest three grand he'd ever earned. Spring half term came and I was off, over to Atlanta again, where Lynda and I had a good week in a city that was almost as cold as Kirkby. I rented a car and drove it the six hours up to Raleigh, where I stayed overnight in a motel dedicated to the needs of the South's travelling salesmen population. I met one of these gentlemen at the "inclusive continental breakfast buffet" and thought I'd landed on a different planet. He spoke English, but was so strange we might as well have spoken Chinese. Getting away from him, I did a written test and an interview at the school district and was informed by phone a day or two later that I had a job starting in August.

Lynda's flat was in a cheap, racially mixed area which reminded me of Whitefield Road in the old days. One afternoon I answered the door to an African American lady who was proselytising on behalf of a local evangelical church. She told me that, "You a grown man and you got sin on you, an' you can only wash that sin away by the blood of our saviour, Jesus Christ."

I thanked her very much and said it was lovely to meet her, but that I was Church of England and hailed from England.

"Where's that?" she asked "ain't that up north some place? 'Cos I know you're American 'cos you speak English"

I told her that yes, I was from up north and she happily went on her way.

Back in Kirkby, one of the footballing teachers asked me if I'd managed to get away anywhere during the half term and I informed him that I'd been to Atlanta, Georgia, driven up to Raleigh, North Carolina and managed to get a job for the new school year. Although he was a little impressed, it was back to business as usual in Ruffwood. Friday night football changed once more to the outdoor pitches and I began to wonder what I was doing going for a third try in the U.S.

At Easter, it was back to Atlanta. Lynda and I drove a hire car up to see her parents in a tiny pueblo in the heart of Illinois, hours away from the nearest city. Her parents were charming and welcomed me, although Lynda had a younger teenage sister who was the epitome of the Yankee brat. Her dad had bought her a new Ford Probe car, which she drove about with disdain towards everyone else on the road. The sister was a perfect example of Americans raising their children to be entitled and smarmy, believing in their own superiority with complete disregard to their own self awareness. Once again, I felt like I'd landed on an alien planet, which would only get worse.

Next morning, being Easter Day, I was expected to attend the Sunrise Service with Lynda's family. I'd attended church many times with my mum at our local church in Anfield, but I wasn't expecting what I witnessed. On entering the Methodist chapel, I saw that a rock band was set up to play, somewhat different to the Church of England, but ok, I had to keep an open mind. We took our seats as the "service" began with a young bloke getting up to testify.

"A year ago, ah was a hopeless drug addict a- smokin' crack, but now thanks to the power of the Lord, ah'm drug free. Praise God almighty, let me hear you say A-men". The congregation responded and the rock band struck up a song. They weren't great, but I persevered. Next, a young woman got up to testify.

"A year ago, I was a-sleepin' around, gittin' myself into trouble, I was even at risk of gittin' AIDS! Nah, thanks to the power of the Lord, ahm celibate! Let me hear y'all say AMEN!" The crowd of rednecks and farmers joined in enthusiastically. A couple more rock songs and thankfully, it was over. Lynda apologised.

"It's not usually like that," she said.

"Amen to that," I replied. I hadn't even realised she was religious, let alone from a family of fundamentalist fanatics. I'd forgotten that this was the middle of nowhere, what people on the east coast called "fly over country", where people's minds had developed in a way quite at odds with European culture, never mind the football obsessed back streets of Scouseland.

August came and I reported for duty in Raleigh. After my encounter in the midwest, I thought I knew it all, but I'd landed in an episode of The Beverly Hillbillies. To be fair, they weren't all rednecks and crackers- the African Americans always seemed a lot more normal to me. At teacher induction, one gentleman, who still seemed to be fighting the Civil War remarked,

"No offence Martin, but they're bringin' in people from England now?" I was offended at his ignorance and prejudice against immigrants. I'd experienced it a couple of times before, but not often.

The school told me that I'd be teaching science, even though I had no science qualification, and they were giving me a classroom, not a lab. When I pointed out that I wasn't a science teacher I was told-

"They're special education students and you're a special education teacher, so you'll be fine."

I was given a set of textbooks at junior school level and was expected to get on with it. I returned said books to the stock room and found a set slightly more advanced, which would at least be credible for high school students. I wasn't going to embarrass my students with age inappropriate content.

I collaborated with the science department and was able to do some basic experiments and a demonstration where the teacher boils the water vapour out of an aluminium petrol can, and it collapses. I did what I could, recording science programmes from cable television for my tenth graders, which they enjoyed. On a personal level, I found a small apartment and bought a white Mazda "Miata" MX5 car. This was all good fun, but I was lonely and once more in a place where I knew nobody. Lynda and I arranged to meet up in Myrtle Beach for Labor Day weekend; I searched through a book which purported to tell the reader how to "do America on a shoestring" and booked a cheap motel in the South's favourite redneck resort…which was a mistake. Arriving there, I realised it made the Bates Motel look like the Waldorf Astoria. Lynda turned up and went mental at my cheapskate mistake. Next day, we switched to the Myrtle Beach Club, a lovely motel which is probably long gone. We lazed on the beach and, at some point, I'd parked the Mazda in a multi storey car park; coming out in the twilight of the early evening, we got mixed up in a car parade. By total chance, university age kids started cheering the brand new MX5, with its pop up headlamps which were then novel and cool. Lynda still looked the part of an undergraduate, whilst at thirty three, I suppose I could have passed for a PhD. student, or a philandering professor.

Back in Raleigh I wanted something to occupy myself between the occasional six and a half hour drive down to Atlanta. I heard that a new school on Leesville Road had just opened, and they were looking for a junior varsity soccer coach, for the lads in 9th and 10th grade. I got over there as fast as possible, met the coach of the varsity squad, a fellow Brit called Paul.

"You're just in time," said my new colleague, a thin, lanky fair haired bloke with a sardonic attitude, who spoke in an indeterminate accent from the south of England; he reminded me to once more refer to football as "soccer". He had the requisite P.E. teacher moustache, which perhaps they handed out at teacher training college in the late 80s.

" They have their first game in two day's time. So, best get stuck in, as they haven't trained at all. Oh, by the way, because we're a new school, we only have students up to 11th grade this year, so I'll be taking the best of your 10th graders for the Varsity squad."

This was akin to the manager being brought in five games before the end of the season, to avoid the drop. Better get on with it, then.

I met the lads and split them into teams to play a match, so I could get an idea of who was who. I wasn't helped by a well meaning local guy, who'd coached some of the lads in a community team, who pointed to various players and tried to explain their strengths, weaknesses and positions. It was too much to take in as I didn't know the boys' names, let alone where to play them. I listened to the helpful advice and 48 hours later, they lined up. Understandably, the game was a disaster- my team was beaten eight nil- and to make matters worse, the advice I'd been given by the local lad was completely wrong. I had to sort this out.

To add to our woes, I was told that the school district couldn't afford a driver for the school bus, so I was expected to pilot the 66 seater vehicle around the Raleigh beltway. Politely, I informed them that they were mental- I didn't have the necessary commercial driver's licence, and I didn't know who did. My erstwhile football advisor reckoned he could drive it, but I passed on that one due to his less than excellent knowledge of our young players. Instead, parents were drafted in to transport the boys to our next game, at Athens Drive High School. Upon arrival at their stadium I was more overawed than I had been at Caesar Rodney; it was a bowl shaped stadium seating 2500 spectators, which they no doubt got for their American Football matches. Our audience was maybe forty parents and friends, so not quite the same atmosphere, although it beat the plastic pitch at Skem or the mud of the Langley estate.

It had been a week since our last match, and I'd sorted the lads into provisional positions. I'd also taught them two things about offside- push up out of defence quickly, and for our fast centre forward (a lad they nicknamed "sticky" due to his lean frame and resemblance to a stick insect) to stay level with the last defender, which was onside at the time. I'd consulted my F.A. handbook, which I'd brought from home, which recommended the long ball game with passes for defence or midfield for strikers to run onto. Things were going well until the wizened referee, an old man wh'do been shrunk to the size of a raisin from too much time in the North Carolina sun, kept flagging "Sticky" offside everytime. He clearly thought the rule was to do with where the player is when the ball is received, not when it is passed. My attacking master plan was failing due to the Good Ole Boys down South not understanding the rules. We lost again but only two nil this time. Things were improving. As we trudged back to our cars, the sun-ripened referee approached me. He was wearing the black and white striped "gridiron" ref's uniform, as the Wake County public schools system obviously didn't stretch to providing him with a kit.

"Your boy tried tah run forward too fast ever' time," he said, "but ah nailed him. I blew mah whistle and nailed him offsides!"

"Yes, thank you, referee." It was no use arguing. Such was the standard of referees' ignorance of the rules that my team refused to pass the ball back to the goalie, which I'd told them was ok, so long as the goalie didn't pick it up. They were quite certain they'd give away a penalty under the auspices of the local officials.

Next up, we travelled to Enloe High, where I was almost sent off after finally snapping with a referee. We were winning, and scored a second goal which was smashed in so hard that it hit the stanchion (which used to support the back of football nets) and bounced out again. The official started to question if it counted as a goal.

"Is that a goal? I'm ain't sure if that counts as a goal," I heard him say.

"YOU DON'T KNOW WHAT YER DOIN'!" I shouted, as I had many times in the Kop when disagreeing with decisions. This time, though, the ref was only feet away. He walked across and I braced myself in case of fisticuffs.

"Sir, if you carry on like that I will dismiss you from the pitch!" he said.

"Yes, ref, but that's a goal, anyone knows that."

"Yes thank you. No more," he replied, keeping his cool where I'd lost mine. He pointed to the centre circle and awarded the goal. I stayed polite for the rest of the game, and we won our first match.

The American school soccer season only runs during the first two months of the autumn, with the state tournament extending into November. Paul knew that he had little chance of the Big Show this time round, with no twelfth graders. Instead, he poached my best lads, including "Sticky", who then sat on the bench due to his lack of physical size against eighteen year old lads on the other teams. I had two secret weapons though; the fattest boy on the team also happened to be the most skilful, being able to pinpoint a pass from thirty yards, but with the obvious disadvantage that, being twenty pounds overweight, he could only move very slowly. I'd been building up the team's fitness with laps of the track, and had given my chubbiest player a diet regime, with the promise that he'd play in the last games of the season if he shed at least ten pounds. He had worked hard, and the lard was melting off him. The other secret weapon was a boy who was known amongst the other lads as perhaps the best player, but he'd broken his arm at the start of the season and had it in a cast. This meant that he couldn't participate at all for at least a month. Now, the dynamic duo were ready to be cast into the cauldron for the last few games.

We began at home against the mighty Athens Drive. I'd told the boys that they were too respectful of our opposition's reputations, and that, mentally, we were defeating ourselves. Our new motto was to be "No respect!", a catch phrase I'd picked up from the American comedian Rodney Dangerfield. The lads kicked off with a new attitude, but went one nil down. I shouted to our goalie, Eric, "Hey, what's our motto?"

He shouted, "NO RESPECT!" and it galvanised the team. A long range pass found our front runners and it was one- one. Our parents were smiling at their sons during the break, and I told the lads to keep getting forward with speed and keeping the pressure on. Ten minutes before the end, Leesville went two one up.

"Go at them!" I shouted. "Don't just defend now, keep playing!"

We held on for a rousing victory against a school with a not inconsiderable local reputation. Another big result, and, as we'd finished a bit quicker, I sauntered over to see the end of the Varsity game. They lost.

Now, after a terrible start, our short season was rolling. We played Wake Forest again, the side that had beaten us eight nil, and this time it was much closer, a score of four two to them. Their coach was complementary about how much we'd improved in a short time. Going into the final game at far away Lee County School, in the town of Sanford- well out of our school district in a more rural area- we had a chance of a 50% record, meaning we'd have won as many games as we'd lost. The boy whose arm was broken had now mended- only a soft, bandaged cast remained- and my slimmed down centre midfield star was all ready. For once, we found a bus driver for the trip, and the lads joked that it was really Lee "Country" School, due to the down home accents of the hayseed hicks we would face.

The game began well and my midfield maestro managed a half, before being winded- he still wasn't fully fit, but he'd sprayed the ball around with unsurpassed accuracy, which my attacking players ran onto, scoring two quick goals. We had a third chance, which was saved, as the lads had followed my coaching too much to the letter. The F.A.

Coaching manual said that, statistically, most goals were scored inside the six yard area, so that's what we had to do. On this occasion my player held onto the ball too long before taking his shot. The Lee County goalie got back and saved it. Indeed, the country boys, for whom "soccer" must, at best, have been a third choice sport, made a good game of it, and at full time the score was five- three in our favour. It was time for the lads to complete an American end of season tradition which had begun in the NFL- dumping the Gatorade container over the coach.

"Thanks, lads!" I shouted, soaking wet but with the memory of my time in North Carolina cemented.

I'd decided not to stay but to return to the school in Kirkby at Christmas, who, it seemed, would welcome me back. I couldn't get used to life in the South, with its Guns and God attitude. I overheard one obese white lady in the teacher's lunch area complaining about regulations around buying handguns.

"Ah went to a gun show on Saturday and ah wanted to buy a gun, but the dealer said ah needed I.D. and there wuz a three day waitin' period. Did you all ever heah of that before, at a goddamn GUN SHOW?" she moaned.

Meanwhile, an armed Deputy Sheriff, a nice but dim lad called Shawn, roamed the corridors ready for any outbreaks of shootin'. I'd been told that a student had brought a gun into school a while back, in his book bag. When he'd thrown the bag on the floor, the gun had gone off. Now, there were metal detectors at every entrance and security guards in the car park, and I didn't really trust Shawn not to shoot himself in the foot. I felt sorry for my students, who had got used to my Scouse-

British accent as I had theirs. One lesson, some rowdy African American boys were chatting in their local street slang.

"I know what you're saying, you know." One of the lads asked me to prove that I knew what the conversation was about and I told him.

"I guess you do understand us. How you know what we wuz sayin'?"

"I listen to a lot of rap music."

"You do? What you listen to, man?"

"Well, I got Public Enemy at the crib," I answered, using my best street talk.

"He said AT THE CRIB! This motherfucker's crazy! Hey, you alright man."

My relationship with Lynda was as strong as ever. We still liked each other just as much, but driving from Raleigh to Atlanta in a tiny Mazda was getting to me. I'd told her that we either had to make plans to be together long term, including planning marriage and moving to one city, or splitting up. She chose the latter and I agreed. Over the final weekend that school finished for the winter break, I drove the MX5 up to Newport News in Virginia, from where it would be shipped straight to Liverpool. I had to wonder if my car would be sad to leave the warmth and sunshine of North Carolina, for the drizzle back home, then thought, don't be bloody stupid, it's a car. At the port, I got a hire vehicle which I drove back to Raleigh, where I slept on the floor in the now empty apartment. Next day it was on to Atlanta and one last night of unbridled passion with Lynda. The fact that I'd never see her again certainly spiced things up and it was quite an evening. Next day, Lynda saw me off at the huge Atlanta terminal building; I turned to go through security without looking back, and that was the last time I ever saw her.

Extra time!

Chapter One

Ey, you're Yaphet Kotto!

It may be a surprise for a chapter heading to be about a lesser known, but highly rated African American actor, but his connection with Liverpool will become clear. Mr. Kotto had starred as the main villain in the James Bond film, *Live and Let Die*, as Dr. Kananga, or Mr. Big. As such, he was imprinted onto the retina of every Scouse thirteen year old boy. Dr. Kananga was quite a busy man, being the dictator of fictional island San Monique, in addition to owning a chain of restaurants in New Orleans and New York called "Fillet of Soul."

Whilst rated only 16th on the all time list of Bond movies, *Live and Let Die* is famous for Yaphet's memorable encounter with racist Sheriff J.W. Pepper in the legendary speedboat chase, and the theme song is by Sir Paul McCartney.

In summer 1990, Yaphet Kotto was in rehearsals for a Bill Kenwright production of a play called *Fences* at the Liverpool Playhouse. Crossing Williamson Square, just as he'd crossed 110th Street in the film of the same name, Yaphet was accosted by a friend of Don Crane - yes, Cranie, who'd famously left a holiday in Corfu early in 1987, to fit carpets in Breck Road. The friend's name was "Fozzer" and he uttered the eternal line-

"Ey, you're Yaphet Kotto! Whorrer yer doin' in Liverpool?"

The well known actor explained that the life of an actor took him worldwide, and it was now his pleasure to grace the stage of Liverpool's finest repertory theatre.

Cranie has significance in our story as he, too, grew up near Havelock Street, although he very much was able to kick a ball down it. Don was a fine footballer well into his middle age and, in the mid 90s, played for the "Old Boys" team of his Alma Mater, the since demolished Collegiate School. Although Don attended the school, it was in name only, as he spent most of his time truanting or suspended: he hated the place, with its constant regime of corporal punishment. Now, the lure of the football field drew him back, and he explained to me, at the beginning of 1994, that the team embarked on an annual tour of the Isle of Man each Easter. It was, he assured me, full of football, frolics and jolly japes, so, now in my mid thirties and too old for 18-30 holidays in Majorca, I agreed that this sounded an attractive proposition, staying as we would be at The Haremount Hotel, the last word in island luxury.

First, though, there was the plastic pitch in Skelmerdale to get back to. Paul, back in Raleigh N.C., had thought I was insane to return to Kirkby, but I explained that constant warmth and sunshine was not necessarily a recipe for happiness. After the end of term sports speeches at Leesville High, he had presented me with a t-shirt bearing the image of a King Mackerel, a large fish often caught off the coast of the Carolinas. I was pleased to be recognised in this way, and wore the shirt regularly whilst drinking lager in The Old Campfield. Skelmerdale showed just how much of a difference 3740 miles can make to the weather, as it was particularly freezing in January and February, but a good runabout shook off the tensions of the week in school. Our headmaster, a Kirkby lad made good who'd succeeded in getting the school into the news, by inviting Princess Anne to turn up (which she did- twice) was a decent footballer and insisted on joining in, although he made sure to get changed separately. It wouldn't do for the minions to see his bare flesh. Our Head was now a plump balding man in his forties, but he could still pass well and get around the pitch a bit.

On a particularly grim night at the beginning of '94, our teachers' team was facing a rough lot of drivers and linesmen from British Rail. Perhaps upset by the upcoming deregulation and splitting up of the railways, they were in no mood to play nice. In the first half I was at left back, and got the full impact of their right winger, who collided with me whilst we went for the same ball. I say we went for the ball, but he didn't have much interest in getting it and broke one of my ribs in the impact. I could feel it had gone, but had no intention of giving him the satisfaction of showing any pain. As the game went on, I could see the attacking skills of our P.E. teachers, and the silky running of the young history teacher on our right wing, were overcoming the brutality of the rail workers. We were a couple of goals up at half time. In their frustration, a wheeltapper or shunter slid into our head teacher and brought him down. To his credit, he was straight up and grabbed the ball for the free kick.

"Giz the ball, yer fat little cunt," said a neanderthal rail worker to our boss. The rest of us were stunned- we'd never heard him spoken to like this.

It was the spur to a wider margin of victory, and we won six -two.

"Not your night," I observed in satisfaction, to the gorilla who'd broken my rib.

Easter came around in relentless fashion and it was time for the first of my four expeditions to the Isle of Man with the Collegiate Old Boys. An interesting bunch, it was impossible to determine just how many had attended the defunct school- the youngest lads must surely have missed its existence. There was a footballing window cleaner named Jim, who was so unsuccessful at his chosen craft that he couldn't afford a van, thus transporting his ladders and buckets by bus. Of the larger-than-life characters, Gerry Prendergast stood out. He was continuing the proud Scouse tradition of shell suit, muzzy and tight dark perm into the nineties, a look which was now dying out elsewhere on Merseyside. To add his own take on things, Gerry had updated the fashion with a small pigtail twisted into the perm at the rear. He spoke in a raspy, breathless voice and told fantastical stories of his exploits at L.F.C. away matches on the continent-

"The police wouldn't let the ship sail from the port, so we waz swingin' across the riggin', fighten 'em, armed to the teeth with Stanley knives." This was the 1980s weapon of favour for Scouse football hooligans, and bovver boys of any ilk. How much of Gerry's stories were true and how much was embellished beyond reality was anyone's guess, but he loved to stand on the touchline, giving advice and taking the piss in rotation.

"How come you don't play yourself, Gerry?" I asked.

He clutched the top left hand side of his shell suit and answered, "bad ticker."

In the first match at Ronaldsway, I decided that, given my experience at Skem and my training runs around Sefton Park, I was now good enough for midfield. I tried to get forward at every opportunity, but the Manx defender was quicker to the ball than me on every occasion. He was good too, winning the ball cleanly.

"Chop him down, Martin," came Gerry's advice from the sideline. Next time I attempted to win the ball, in came the defender again, only this time I didn't pull out when he'd already won the tackle. I kicked him hard on the shin, in an almost exact repeat of how I'd been kicked myself at Langley School ten years earlier. To his credit, the other bloke didn't even flinch, just took his free kick and got on with it. I apologised at the end.

"That was funny when you kicked that fella, Mart," complimented Cranie. I was just thankful to get substituted at half time.

Next day we were at St. John's, a beautiful ground in the middle of the island, near to Tynwald hill, where the Manx parliament had originally met. It was in a glade that sheltered it from the wind, in contrast to Ronaldsway; it seemed like the Isle of Man government had chosen to build their airpost in the windiest spot on the island. For some reason, this bucolic idyll raised my spirits and I decided that the St. John's team was rubbish, so of course, any sport being 50% mental,(some estimates say 80%) I played much better. I laid on a pass for Cranie and another for a tall bloke called Frank… a completely different Frank to the Rufwood drama teacher who had now moved on, perhaps back to treading the boards.

Back at the Haremount Hotel, I noticed that each floor had its own full size fire hose.

"Ey lads, yer fancy doin' a bit of Backdraftin'?" Gerry enquired, referring to the then current film about American firefighters. I declined, saying that this probably wouldn't be a good idea. He was attempting to rekindle his youthful endeavours. Cranie retired to his room for a short kip before dinner and, when I came to wake him up two hours later, found him unconscious on his bed, eyes wide open and not appearing to breathe.

"CRANIE! DON! WAKE UP!" I panicked. I had the hotel phone in my hand, ready to ask them to call emergency services as we had a cardiac arrest situation. Then Cranie stirred.

"Sorry, Mart, just fell asleep there."

"You had your eyes open and weren't breathing!" I was all shook up, but Don was unmoved.

"Yeah, just a quick nap. Is it time for dinner?" I said it was and we went down to the carvery, all you can eat for a tenner. Don proceeded to try to put them out of business by eating several platefuls, then went up for dessert.

Slicing off a piece of cake, he inspected it closely, changed his mind, said "Fuck it," put the slice back and took the rest of the cake, which he ate with gusto.

Back in Kirkby, I enquired of Dave, head of P.E. you'll remember, if he could suggest any coaching courses for me to attend. I still had my trusty F.A. coaching manual, and earlier in the term I'd brought it along to a training session with my new year 9 team. My team wasn't doing so well this time, so I decided to teach them the Cruyff turn, a move that the book explained in a series of diagrams, which made it appear easy. I lined the lads up.

"OK lads, so this is the Cruyff turn. This will make a big difference to our season." I tried to demonstrate the move, then realised I'd forgotten it. No matter, the training manual was there and I had a quick read. The lads stood patiently.

"OK lads, this is actually how it's done" I said, as the ball flew away from me and landed in some mud ten yards away. The team watched on, clearly unimpressed.

"Actually, lads, the Cruyff turn isn't that important after all. Let's just have a game of five a side."

In early June, after the season and the Isle of Man tour was concluded, I drove to Edge Hill College (now a university in its own right) for the coaching training, which began on a Sunday morning at 9.00 a.m. Approaching the entrance, I pulled over for a second to get my bearings, and moments later, a second car joined me.

"Excuse me, mate, is this where the football is?" I recognised the bloke as a Liverpool F.C. player.

"Yes, there's a football course here but I think it's a different one to the one you want," I told him.

I parked up and, after a bit of wandering, found the correct building. A coach, who seemed in charge, was already lecturing away to a bunch of fellas, who generally looked fitter and tougher than me. Amongst them I spotted the professional player whom I'd just met and I recalled his name. Mark Walters had played a couple of games for England, in addition to playing for The Reds.

"Excuse me, am I in the right place?" I enquired.

"What's yer name, lad?" I told him. "Yes, yer on the list. F.A. Preliminary Coaching badge. You're ten minutes late. Don't be late again."

Dave had stitched me up by putting me on a course which was the first step to professional football players becoming professional managers. Most of the other participants were amateurs but could at least play. There was one other pro player, a beefy lad from Bolton Wanderers, whom I recognised.

The first exercise was on passing the ball around in a group. I got in the middle and was intended to intercept the ball, which I couldn't, no matter how I huffed and puffed. Mark Walters, seeing my agony, said " This guy's knackered," stepped into the middle and brought the ball under control first time, by raising his right leg level with his head. Wow. I'd never seen professional skills up close; my fellow amateurs were equally impressed.

Throughout the course, I couldn't get away from Mark- maybe he'd decided to look after me, as he'd observed that I couldn't play, but it had the opposite effect of making me nervous. The time came for me to coach a small group of players, and there was Mark again, with the Bolton player this time. I started explaining what I wanted them to do in a teacherly manner, when the boss stepped in.

"Look, I told you not to give a lecture, just get them started doing something. The weather is usually freezing during the season." I felt like a complete dickhead.

Next day it happened again. I had to defend against someone in a practice match and guess what? I had to mark Mark. Again, he was terribly humble, but I just said,

"Look, Mark, I'm not even going to try to tackle you. I'm a big clumsy bastard and I don't want you getting injured in a stupid way when we need you to play for Liverpool." Mark nodded in agreement.

Later in the week we were required to come back for a written exam on tactics and the laws of the game, which I passed with ease. Thankfully, there was no question on the Cruyff turn. I waited another couple of weeks before an A4 envelope arrived at my flat, with a certificate of attendance at the course, but saying that, overall, I had failed due to my inability to kick a ball in any controlled manner. At least I'd made friends with Mark Walters.

Time sped past like it had for Rod Taylor in the 1960 film *The Time Machine* ; Christmas, winter, spring and time again for the Isle of Man. The familiar faces were back, and we were sitting in the Piano Lounge at The Haremount Hotel. A posh bird in a posh frock was singing a song, and when she finished, she came across to our area. Although she spoke with an upper crust accent, every other word from her was "fuck". Perhaps she was attempting to send us a message, although I was unsure. One of our lot, an ageing gentleman who had once played for Everton, leant across and requested-

"Ey love, could yer stop swearin'? We're not used to that kind of language." Absolutely correct; we were gentlemen of the highest calibre, right down to the lad who stayed in a cheap guest house, only to bunk into the Haremount for his full Manx breakfast, complete with kippers, every day.

In 1995, the Collegiate squad was reduced to 14 playing members; Gerry was still there to barrack from the sidelines. In our first game that

Easter, he commented that, when we were losing, "They really knew we'd thrown the towel in when we put Martin on." Cranie chipped in with the comment that "it wasn't a holiday, it was a quest," and my services, at the age of 35, were required for four of the six games. My most memorable moment came at Laxey on a dreary Easter Sunday, as the great feat of Victorian engineering known as the Laxey Wheel, the largest working water wheel in the world, chugged away in the background. The football was as dreary as the weather and we were all pretty knackered by that stage. Late in the game, seeing danger from a Laxey F.C. attack, I raced back into the penalty area to attempt a goal line clearance, only for the ball to bounce off my knee and into the goal. All I wanted was for the great water wheel to swallow me up and to disappear from the earth, so ashamed was I. Completely out of proportion to the importance of the game, I thought my teammates would never let me live it down, but since then I've seen many "oggies" scored in professional games, and everyone accepted that it was an accident…although there was some vigorous piss taking afterwards, I'd scored in the Isle of Man, just not at the right end.

The Everton v. Tottenham F.A. Cup semi final had taken place that same weekend, 9th April 1995, the same year that The Toffees went on to win the trophy. Cranie and I were in the Stakis Casino, the island's night-life hot-spot, with some of our teammates. Don enjoyed an occasional flutter, usually chucking away his money on roulette, but this time it was Black Jack. He came back ten minutes later and said-

"Ey Mart, go and talk to the fella over there. He says his name is Boris, and he's the biggest tit I've ever met in me life. I told him I have my own casino in Liverpool, and he believed it. "

He pointed towards an overweight, hunched, ball-shaped figure with a mop of blonde hair on his head. "Go and talk to Mart, he's hilarious."

I went across for a chat. Compared to the posh bird who we'd heard singing and swearing in the Piano Bar the night before, this bloke made her sound common. Boris had the plummiest public school accent I'd ever heard, to the extent that it sounded as if he was putting it on for a joke. He was tolerant as I bullshitted away until I got bored of it. Only twenty five years later did I realise I'd been taking the piss from our future prime minister, Mr. Johnson, but there was no problem with that. He got his revenge by taking the piss out of the whole country.

There is a montage of other memories from the island tours of 1994-97. In one scene in the picturesque village of Kirkmichael on the north side of the island, Geoff, a mate of Don's, saw the ball looping towards him. Knowing what Geoff would attempt, Cranie shouted "Don't try it!" but it was too late. Geoff had volleyed the ball before it had touched the ground, slotting it into the upper left hand corner of the net. In another scene at Peel F.C. , Collegiate had put me and another clumsy footed bloke up front to at least give us a run. My fellow forward was called Tony and he was of Italian descent, but the others had decided that, in the same tradition as Iron Eyes Cody, a Sicillian actor who made a living from playing Native American characters, Tony bore a striking resemblance to Chiricahua Apache leader, Cochise. This was then shortened in the Scouse manner, so that Tony became "Coach", a nickname he quite enjoyed. Coach and I hadn't seen much of the ball in the first half and I was getting somewhat annoyed by this. A young Peel F.C. player had trapped the ball arrogantly in midfield, and was now taunting one of our lads to take it from him. I sprinted across, dragged the ball back from under his foot, turned and ran towards the goal. As the keeper came out towards me, I shouted "Coach!" and passed him the ball. Tony shot five yards wide of the goal— but despite the fact that we were both offside, it was a great moment.

On one of the tours, a bright spark in the Collegiate management thought it would be a brilliant idea to have an "international" match against the Island under 21 team, as the IOM is a bailiwick of the UK, not technically part of it. Thus, it is a tax haven for the rich. The match was arranged for the Douglas Bowl, a magnificent arena with a capacity of 3350 spectators- even dwarfing Athens High School's impressive stadium- which is reserved for top sporting fixtures on the island. Somehow, the idea that this was a serious International fixture took root, and posters appeared, announcing Liverpool Collegiate v. Island under 21 XI, printed on the neon poster paper of yore. Gerry, Coach and I hadn't been selected- no surprise there- but Don, Geoff, Frank and a Cockney lad called Mark, who certainly hadn't gone to school at the Collegiate, were set to take their places on the pitch. I noted that they were even charging admission so, whilst I searched my pocket for the requisite amount, I asked a local who he thought would win.

"Aye, it'll be Liverpool. I don't think our lads have much of a chance against them." He and others had only read the word "Liverpool" and were expecting to see the LFC team thrash their young hopefuls. It didn't exactly go that way, though, as some of our passes went astray and were intercepted by the fleet footed Island youths. Quickly, they were one nil up. On the left wing, Mark the Cockney attempted a long kick and instead the ball bounced past him in a manner I was usually the master of. There was an audible gasp from the crowd, and I thought, this is going to end up twenty nil to them, a score I'd endured in parks or hollers as a 1960's kid. Thankfully, Collegiate rallied and only lost a somewhat respectable five- one. I think Geoff may have scored our only goal.

By this time it was the latter half of the nineties and I'd left Ruffwood, presented with a beer tankard for my efforts on the field. I was grateful to my fellow teachers for this gesture. I moved to the local school for students with Social, Emotional and Behavioural Difficulties. I'd fulfilled my early dream of working in a "sin bin", as the nice lady had described it, but it wasn't exactly what I'd expected. Many of the children were imbued with a level of violence I'd never seen before, and restraints were a daily occurrence. I tried to stay positive and keep an outlook that I was, as the Midwest Methodists would have described it, "doin' the Lord's work", but it's not always easy to feel that way when you're being verbally abused most of the day. I went home feeling mentally tired all the time, but I still had the physicality of a young man; when I got told by a doctor, after an Isle of Man tour in 1997, where I'd twisted my knee- he explained that it was a hinge joint, not a universal joint, and perhaps I should think about stopping football- I took no notice. I did stop going to the Island after that, but I decided, as I'd done at Langley in 1984, the best way to win the trust of the students was to play football with them. A male teaching assistant, a Kirkby native, rented two outdoor five a side pitches for us at Kirkby Sports centre, and we made it a weekly thing. I was glad to have the teaching assistant with me, who, coincidentally, told me that my attempt to teach the Cruyff turn had now become a thing of local legend.

After my first term at the school I moved across to teach years 5 and 6, thus reprising my role in West Yorkshire from the late 80s. I taught the students how to read, how to control their emotions, and a much wider variety of maths than simple arithmetic. I even taught them chess, until this went awry when I realised that none of them could accept losing. Of course, we had football every week out on the field, when I could stop the lads from fighting amongst themselves long enough to play. We had a Variety Club coach which I used, with one of my great female classroom assistants (actually, they were all great) to take a team up to the SEBD school at the other end of the borough in Halewood, to play a match. Both teams being equal, the matches were played out in an equitable manner, with a draw usually engineered to placate both sides.

Somehow, my erstwhile friend Derek, the PE teacher from the learning difficulties school in Huyton, got wind that we had a team, and left a message with our receptionist to ask whether he could bring his juniors to play against us.

"Of course," I told our receptionist/ secretary, another person of whom I have fond memories, as adversity bonds you together. The match was arranged for a week or so ahead, and Derek turned up, looking a little greyer and more weatherbeaten, but still with the requisite muzzy. As his players got off their corresponding Variety Club minibus, it looked like something was awry.

"Excuse me, Derek," I enquired. "Aren't these boys a little large for juniors?"

"What? Oh, maybe. They feed them well in Huyton," he laughed.

Derek's boys were at least a year older and bigger than our diminutive year five and sixes. The match proceeded and of course, we were thrashed. Derek drove off with a supercilious smirk. Right, I thought, if that's how you want to play it, fair enough.

I arranged the return fixture a fortnight later and this time I came prepared. There wasn't a junior kid in the squad; they were all year sevens with a smattering of year eight lads, and, for good measure, I brought along Marvin, a year nine boy who looked destined to become a future heavyweight champion boxer. Derek was refereeing and couldn't keep up, as my team of ringers danced circles round his lot. Marvin stood on the sidelines as an unused sub.

"Can I go on now, Sir?"

"No, it's OK Marvin. I think we've embarrassed them and their teacher enough."

Derek never again phoned up for another match.

At Easter 1998, I wasn't going to the Isle of Man. Instead, I was getting married to my second wife Helen, whom I'd met at Ruffwood where she worked in the offices. My marriage was to be the longest and happiest relationship of my life; we split up after eighteen years in total, of dating and matrimony. To celebrate the end of term, I organised a junior football tournament, and to present the trophy, I asked the children in my class to write letters to former England and Liverpool star, Phil Thompson. Unlike today, a player who'd appeared 42 times for England and had won multiple trophies with Liverpool-including once thinking that he'd lost the European Cup in a Kirkby pub after winning it in Rome- did not retire a millionaire. The art of football punditry had not yet been invented, so, like many ex players, Phil had set up his own business. It was called Phil Thompson's Pine DIY, and anyone could wander into the shop to meet the former football star quite freely. It was to this address that I mailed the childish letters, asking Phil to present the trophy to the tournament winners at our school. Sure enough, his secretary got in touch and said that Phil would be happy to oblige.

I had no intention of winning the tournament and instead it was a P.R. stunt to improve our relationship with neighbouring schools. One mainstream junior school sent along their year five team, who were much better than everyone else; there were four teams on who played a round-robin system, and they came out on top. Mr. Thompson stood on the steps outside my classroom and presented the trophy, which had been donated by Radcliffe taxis, who had the contract for bringing our students to school. It was quite a handsome pot. When Phil had finished speaking, our head teacher gave me a nudge and said "make a speech thanking him".

I'd quite forgotten to do this, but managed to say a bumbling thank you to our star attendee, who'd finished his speech by saying, "Don't forget kids, tell yer dads and grandads, buy all yer wood from us!"

Next day, I drew glares from Billy Radcliffe, taxi man supreme and former colleague of my dad on the Liverpool Hackney Carriages.

"Why didn't you thank me for the trophy?"

"Er, I forgot Bill, but thanks."

So now, decades later and posthumously, once again, thanks for the trophy, Billy Radcliffe. It was a good tournament.

Chapter Two

Fatherland

There comes a time in a man's life, when, if he's lucky, he becomes a father. If he's very, very lucky, he's able to financially support his family in a modest way and provide for his family's welfare and wellbeing. After being promoted to Head of Special Needs at a mainstream school in Wigan in 1999, my daughter came along. We lived in a modern semi detached house and were ecstatically happy. Helen and I, with baby daughter in tow, were able to holiday in Fuerteventura in February 2000. With everything going so well we decided to throw caution to the wind and have another child. Alastair was born in November 2000 and the family was growing. I now fancied myself such a big shot that I decided we should all move to a bigger, detached house. The deciding factor was that three of the four bedrooms had sinks, a middle class feature that had so impressed me whilst dating my university girlfriend, Gill.

In May 2001 I stood at the Childwall Fiveways as the L.F.C. team came past on the traditional open top bus victory parade, with the usual sunny weather that obliges for such occasions. Ranting away to the two year old on my shoulders, who was enjoying the excitement of being carried about, I got some baffled stares from women who realised the impossibility of philosophising loudly on the team's triumph to a child who was only just able to name mum, dad, baby and some other one and two syllable words. By May 2005 however, four years older, both children were able to understand Liverpool's dire situation at half time in the UEFA Champions League Cup final. It was a despondent bedtime which turned to joy for us and millions of other fans world wide. We aimed for our traditional spot outside my mum's house this time, but traffic was so bad that we had to give up, park our car and walk across to Queen's Drive Fire Station. Six year old Lizzie understood it all at this stage, and was delighted when Sami Hyppia waved and smiled at her. He became her favourite player.

It was time for little Alastair to begin his footballing journey in the local under fives football organisation, which was run, surprisingly enough, by an amiable fellow called Dave. Several teams from each age group played in a public park with pitches on the side of the famed Camp Hill, near to where John Lennon grew up with his Auntie Mimi. On the morning of the first match, a group of dads (the collective noun is a "khaki" of dads due to their bland clothing choices) gathered with the sons, and shouted to make themselves heard about how the team should line up. Armchair managers every one, I had the impression that some of them may have called in their opinions to Radio Merseyside's post match football phone-ins, sharing their ill informed ideas.

"What we need is wing backs," suggested one genius, and attempted to explain the wing back system to the little boys, who just stared at him.

"Let's just stick to good old 4-4-2" suggested another, whilst another gentleman, in all seriousness, suggested the "inverted Christmas tree formation." We sent our tiny sons out and, inevitably, it was twenty two five year olds running after the ball, in a repeat of my Dwerryhouse Lane days, a lamented playing field which had now become a housing estate.

I had kept my mouth closed about talking over as the team's coach/manager as I thought I'd done my fair share and it was time to let someone else have a go. A particularly aged looking dad and a slightly more athletic looking bloke offered to run things, which improved slightly. I offered my opinion that the boys should learn some basic skills, and suggested a few things which I'd picked up on my failed F.A. course in 1994. The lads eventually began to spread out a bit on the field. One kid, who seemed particularly hyperactive, had been selected as goalkeeper. He had amazing flexibility and performed the admirable feat of kicking the ball backwards over his head and into his own goal, a trick he performed several times that season. Once, the ball didn't quite trickle in, so a diminutive defender gave it a final tap in for his first oggie. I recalled my own goal at Laxey and despaired for some of the little boys, whose dads were firmly convinced that they were the next Wayne Rooneys. They were a highly competitive lot, some of them shouting aggressively from the sidelines-

"Slide in! Yeah, go on, break his leg son!" and other similar words of helpful encouragement. One father told his son-

"Score a goal or I'll batter yer", whilst another one imparted the fact that, although there was no official league, he'd been keeping tabs on the results and knew "our" position in the unofficial standings.

I could see the madness of the fathers, who were taking all the fun out of the game for their children. They were trying to live out what they were unable to do through their boys, forgetting that decades ago, like me, they'd kicked a ball around just for fun. At the end of the season, I asked organiser Dave if I could start a new team with the ethic of fun and enjoyment. He replied that yes, there were some boys on the waiting list, enough to do just that. I gave the team the daftest name I could think of, in honour of Hamilton Academical, as it's difficult to get a football chant going with eight syllables in the team's name. The emphasis was on skills and learning; Dave and I placed a rope at the side of the pitch to stop frenzied dads from encroaching as they offered personalised coaching advice. I explained the philosophy of the team which was to develop the lads, give everyone a fair chance and equal playing time and not to worry too much about winning at this stage. On this basis we had a jolly season with not too many wins but progress made- the Academicals weren't the best but neither were they the worst. The dads, and some mums, were on phone contacts; one bloke called me to thank me for making the season a positive experience for him and his son.

Our family took a late summer holiday in Cornwall and on the way back, that same bloke called me. Luckily, Helen was driving that stretch so I was able to take the call.

"Martin? Where 'ave yer been lad? The season's started." I explained we'd been on holiday.

"Yer better get back. Dirk Mone has taken over, and he's makin' a mess of things."

He explained that Dirk, a particularly loud mouthed parent who bossed his son relentlessly, had stepped in and had brought back all the bad habits. Sure enough, my first Saturday back, there was Dirk, huffing about in his trackie with the idea firmly fixed in his head that he was Alex Ferguson. He reluctantly let me get things back to how I wanted, but was permanently on my shoulder offering advice, which I ignored. One early autumn Saturday morning, the Academicals turned out for another game with Alastair upfront. I'd noticed that Al had really begun to get the idea of things and had scored once or twice. Dirk's son was on the bench in the first half, and I intended to switch him in for Alastair in the second period. Immediately, there was Dirk on my shoulder.

"Why isn't Ivan playing? Why isn't he up front? He's good, y'know. He can score goals, our Ivan can. Go on, put him on, put him on. It's his birthday, y' know."

"Ivan's going on in the second half, swapping with Alastair."

"Yeah but put him on NOW, put him on, go on, go on." Dirk was the world's most annoying parent. The second half came and Ivan swapped with Alastair, who'd really enjoyed his half. Immediately the Academicals conceded a goal, nothing to do with Ivan.

"Look, they've scored. If Ivan had been on from the start, that wouldn't have happened, that wouldn't."

"DIRK, if you think you can do better, YOU HAVE A GO!" It was the old offering- the -whistle to the moaner, who would then realise that he didn't want to do it trick. To my horror, Dirk said,

"Right! I will! I will take over!" I'd inadvertently given him the chance he relished. Oh no. I'd messed up big time.

We endured three weeks of despondency with Dirk in charge. His favourite bit of advice for the lads was the mnemonic-

"When in doubt, hit it out."

All the good things we'd worked on went out the window. Dave, the head man, had sent a young aspiring coach and referee on an F.A. coaching short course, which had become more accessible over the last ten years or so, and the young guy was attached to our team for help and guidance. He told Dirk that boys shouldn't play in the same position every week so that they could learn more about the game at this early age, and that they should keep learning skills. Dirk disagreed.

"No, they stick to the same positions. Now let's play five a side." There was a collective groan. Later, I went to see Dave who said it was difficult with Dirk, as he worked with him in his job and didn't want to cause discord. I asked the other dads to get in touch with Dave, we had a meeting with Dirk and, a week or two later, the latter bowed to pressure and relinquished the reins to a bloke who, it seemed, could play a bit. He practised corners with the boys and organised things well. All the time though, there was Dirk, on his shoulder and snapping at his heels, waiting to get in again. After several more weeks, the new bloke quit and there, once again was Dirk.

Alastair and I agreed that it was all simply madness. I said that I'd never enjoyed standing on the touchlines on winter mornings… he replied by agreeing that he hadn't enjoyed it much either. We decided to give rugby a go. Down on Aigburth Road was a team run by my old friends, The Collegiate, a school which had now ceased to exist thirty years ago. There was no Garry, Don or Frank, as they were still going to the Isle of Man each Easter, repeating their attempts to relive their youths. The rugby parents were polite and welcoming, didn't encroach on the pitch, didn't encourage their sons (and one daughter) to be violent and didn't threaten their own children with dire consequences if they failed to score a try. The set- up was structured, with different skills taught each year, not a free- for- all; Alastair and I enjoyed it for two years before he'd had enough. The football and rugby he'd played meant that, by the time he got to St. Margaret's secondary school, he didn't have to play on the sloping pitch, if it had still existed. Sometimes, he was promoted to the top group but, he said, this was too much effort, so happily dropped down again to be with his mates. By this time, the sadistic P.E. teachers had all disappeared, but, if we went to school in the 1970s we all had them, didn't we?

Next door to my mum, a woman who'd lived there since she'd moved in as a teenager with her dad, now had some boys of her own. One of the three was in the same school year as Lizzie, except that his birthday was in October 1999, rather than April. The boy's father apparently lived in London and visited infrequently, but he'd had the front garden paved so that the lads could play football. This inevitably meant that the ball would bounce into my mum's garden, and one of the lads would knock and mutter those well known lines-

"Can we have our ball back, please?"

In the back garden, various balls would fly over the fence and, on weekend afternoons round at my mum's with the kids, I'd throw them all back over. The boys were a polite lot who seemed to play football ceaselessly; my mum grew fond of them. Perhaps because their dad wasn't around too much, working in London, there was no aggressive male presence to spoil the sheer fun of kicking a ball, and maybe that's why they were naturals. Taking the lads to a half term coaching camp one October, the lady next door was surprised that her son had been spotted by L.F.C. coaching scouts, and was invited to train with one of their junior squads, where he did very well. Some years later, my mum told me that the family had moved out, as her neighbour had explained to her that there would be press coming round frequently to photograph one of the lads, as he had excelled in the Academy team. They were moving to St. Helens.

The lad in question was Trent Alexander Arnold, which goes to show that, whilst some Scousers can't kick a ball down Havelock Street, some very much can.

Conclusion and acknowledgements

Thank you to my daughter Lizzie, who encouraged me to finish "Kicking a Ball" after putting it aside for 23 years. Life got in the way. She even wrote an article about the legendary status of the unfinished manuscript. Thanks to Alastair for now standing on The Kop alongside me and wearing the famous red shirt to support our team. My grandad and Uncle Bill, who made me a Red, have long gone, but we repeat the tradition thanks to tickets from a friend-of-a-friend. That's how most people get L.F.C. tickets nowadays.

Thanks to the Writing On The Wall Project in Toxteth Library, which encourages local writers. They showed me that all things are possible. Also, thanks to all the characters who appeared in the book. Some are real, some are not. You made the story of my life what it is.

www.ingramcontent.com/pod-product-compliance
Lightning Source LLC
Chambersburg PA
CBHW031353040426

42444CB00005B/270